GIRLS JUST WANNA HAVE FUND$

GIRLS JUST WANNA HAVE FUND$

Four Steps to Financial Freedom

Monica Allen

Girls Just Wanna Have Fund$: Four Steps to Financial Freedom

Hardcover ISBN: 978-1-5445-3573-9
Paperback ISBN: 978-1-5445-3574-6
Ebook ISBN: 978-1-5445-3575-3

Cover design and illustrations: Brandon Michael Allen

To my mom, Betty, the best money manager I know. You deserve part of the credit for anyone this book helps. To my husband, Brad, who has supported me wholeheartedly through all of my endeavors. Finally, to my dear friend Billsy, you left way too soon, but you always looked out for the underdog, especially if it was a pretty girl. You, me, and Mia were an unbeatable team. The Three Amigos strike again!

Finally, this book is dedicated to helping women.

Contents

Introduction

I COULDN'T BELIEVE MY EYES. OH WAIT—YES. YES, I COULD.

I'd come home late, as usual, from my job as a clinical nurse specialist. There was nothing planned for supper.

"Just order a pizza," my husband, Brad, suggested. He was also tired. His job in manufacturing was eating up more hours in his day, too.

"Okay, pizza it is," I said, instinctively reaching for my checkbook. I knew our account was low already. There were some bills that needed to clear, and that's when I saw it. We were so strapped, living paycheck-to-paycheck, that we were unable to buy a pizza. If I ordered pizza, I would have to dip into our tiny savings account.

Why do I have to wait until Friday just to order a pizza? I thought, tensing up. Brad could see it in my body language.

"That bad?" he asked. I nodded.

It was always "that bad." It was like this every week, of every month, of every year, for several years. We were living the American Dream, right? With our two decent salaries, we built a house, filled it with furniture, added two car payments, and soon enough, we had four kids who needed care while we worked for those two decent salaries. Our dual incomes were necessary to keep it all together and functioning. Our family made do with a frozen pizza that night, and I just kept wondering, *Is this all there is?*

I thought I was going to be rich when I got out of college and landed my nursing job. When Brad and I married, I thought with our two incomes, we would be able to do whatever we wanted, whenever we wanted. Instead, we both arrived home after working long shifts, and we couldn't afford to eat out, carry out, or have it delivered.

We ate later than usual that night. I cleaned up the kitchen while Brad got the kids in the tub and into bed, both of us knowing that we'd do another round of the exact same thing tomorrow...and the next day... and the next. When we turned in later that night, both of us were kind of quiet and feeling discouraged.

This is the last time this is going to happen. That mantra floated in my mind as I finally drifted off to sleep.

What Is Financial Bondage?

Financial bondage is like an invisible noose or weight around the neck. Its heaviness stays with you all the time; you are always aware of its presence. The stress and anticipation of the next bill scheduled to arrive is like a migraine trying to peck its way through, and the slightest little upset makes you feel like crying.

The night we couldn't order a pizza was the last straw for me. Something had to change—or the life that I had dreamed of, and worked hard for, was going to disappear.

It had finally hit me: *I need to take complete control of the family finances.*

I didn't know what changes to make at first, but I knew it had to start with me, simply because I was determined to figure this stuff out. I started reading everything I could get my hands on about debt and money management, and we started implementing the changes pretty quickly. I practiced a "fake it 'til you make it" happy attitude, even when my family wasn't quite on board with some of my decisions (we'll get into some of those later).

It's not like people intentionally set out for financial ruin, but we can set ourselves up for it. We start by borrowing from Peter to pay Paul, which buys us some time to figure things out, and that can work for a little while. But then it really takes hold when it's no longer working. Suddenly Peter is charging you late fees, and your checks to Paul are bouncing, at forty bucks a pop. The race is on. You are checking your balance online twice daily, wondering which scenario will win: if you'll make it until payday, or if the check you wrote will clear too early and add an extra forty dollars to your growing deficit.

You might even love your job, but if you're like a high percentage of others, you don't. Either way, it is just a means to an end, because you have to have that paycheck. For me, it was deposited every two weeks, and I knew all of it would get sucked out by debt. It was a balancing act, a horse race, and turmoil just about any time we incurred unexpected expenses.

If you're a homeowner, you were likely told what sort of house payment you could afford—because no lender would loan you more than you could afford, right? A few mortgage payments in, you realize that they never asked about your other bills, or whether your children attended private school, or if you enjoy having furniture or eating. Finally, it dawns on you that in America, you can outspend and outborrow any income.

I know what it feels like to have that underlying stress all the time, where any little thing could make you explode. Or any peace you might glimpse, like watching your kids play in the park, is interrupted by wondering if the electric bill payment will clear. You can't be fully present anywhere, or find much joy, because that weight, that burden of financial bondage, clamps down on you hard.

The psychological effects of financial bondage stay wrapped in that constant underlying stress, where any little thing can disrupt your applecart. My kids used to call it my "monkey freakout," like an angry chimpanzee that rages and jumps around. And believe me, when we were struggling, I had a few of them. I am not one who curses or anything like that, but they didn't like it when I got that way. They would tell each other, "Don't do anything to upset Mom, or she's going to do a monkey freakout."

I just felt like I couldn't really enjoy life or stop the monkey freak-outs from happening when the stress reached a boil. Our bondage was ever-present in my mind, and I couldn't go anywhere or fully enjoy anything because it always reminded me that we were still trapped. I was there, but never fully present.

I did not realize just about everyone lives this way, until I found a way out by gleaning parts and pieces of different financial plans, and started coaching others. Their toys may be newer, their vacations more extravagant, and their clothes more expensive, but many people are scraping by, day-to-day, just like everybody else. I think we have been fooled into thinking that this is the way it has to be—with all this stress on your shoulders, the heaviness of the burden, the pit in your stomach—and you just wake up every day like that, feeling powerless (or worse, not even knowing that you feel that way, and just thinking, *this is how life is*).

You have moments of hope, thinking it is going to be different with your next paycheck, unexpected tax return, or raise...but unless you do something different, it doesn't change.

It Didn't Start with a Pizza

I totally get what it means to start from scratch. In many respects, my life was tracking in ways that set me up for failure, and, in certain instances, society was more than happy to assist in my ruin. I was the second of four kids in a Catholic middle-class family and I had a happy, healthy childhood. I maintained good grades, stayed very involved in school activities, and enjoyed my social life.

When I was sixteen, my busy, go-getter life caught up with me; I found out I was going to be an unwed mother. Some would consider this a major setback, but looking back, it might have been the best thing that could have happened to me. My only daughter was born during spring break of my junior year of high school. Yes, having a baby at such a young age was a major, grow-up-fast event, but it made me realize that there was more to consider than just myself...and that I might not be able to depend on a partner to help me support the family. If I was going to provide the lifestyle that I wanted for my daughter and myself, I was going to have to buckle down in order to get it.

It is no secret that, statistically, teenage mothers have a very low success rate when it comes to graduating college—2 percent, to be exact. In 2014, the National Conference of State Legislatures used census data to conclude that teen pregnancy affects graduation rates. Only 40 percent of teen mothers had finished high school, and fewer than 2 percent had finished college by age 30.

I was very fortunate that my mom and dad assisted me for the next two years until my father unexpectedly died of a heart attack. While it didn't take long for things to grow very lean, financially, in our household, my mother remained my biggest supporter. She babysat for me and somehow seemed to handle the finances easily, but I never fully understood how. She was, and is, the best money manager I know, perhaps from avoiding debt and living within her means. You do not get this knowledge from osmosis, though—someone has to teach you. Many of us do not want to be taught, however, so hopefully we can learn from our own mistakes. Turns out life experience taught me the most.

About three years into college, I thought I had met the man of my dreams. Less than a year after we married, I went through a divorce that I never wanted—being Catholic, you don't get divorced—but when one person in the marriage wants out, you do not have much choice. After we broke up, I found out I was pregnant with his child. Our son was born in January. I returned to college one week later and graduated with my bachelor's degree in May of that year.

I began working as a registered nurse for $9.95 an hour, and felt like I had hit the jackpot! Soon, my heart became restless and I was offered the opportunity to continue my studies and become a psychiatric clinical nurse specialist, a new program for health professionals. When I visited the campus, I discovered they had a traineeship that would pay for my education and included a $500 monthly stipend in exchange for working in their office twenty hours a week. This was an opportunity to get in on the ground floor of a brand-new industry. I was living in subsidized housing, and my landlord agreed to let me remain there. Doors were opening everywhere, and while they were scary, I just needed to be willing to walk through them.

Why would a single, college-educated mother with two young children go back to school? From the outside looking in, I was giving up a steady job in a solid industry to take a chance on a relatively new area. Even if one of your biggest supporters says that your epiphany is "the dumbest thing they ever heard of" because you are already making good money, you have to proceed with what you know is best. You have to listen to wise counsel, but follow your own heart. That's exactly what I set out to do.

There may be people you love and those you want to impress who do not agree with a course you have chosen, or a door that has opened for you, like getting out of debt and living differently than other people. Don't be angry or annoyed with your usual supporters if this happens; they may be scared for you, or scared of the unknown. That's okay—they want to make sure you are looking at it from all sides. Take their input and move forward with love. Go forth and do what is best for yourself and your family. Each person is responsible for living their own life, after all. My point is that if you want your circumstances to change, then you have got to do something different. In time, your hard work will pay off and you will be able to bless others.

Everyone has their story, and I love hearing them. When we know someone's story, it makes a difference; we have a window to look through that explains behaviors and even reveals things that are hidden to casual observers. We no longer look at "perfect" people with envy; we no longer judge a person down on their luck, or look at them with disinterested pity. When we truly listen from the heart, we are less likely to say, "I don't like that person."

For those of us who are in a season of struggle, these stories can also provide us hope. Eventually, I *did* meet the guy of my dreams—Brad—and we have a beautiful family, complete with grandchildren. Our struggles didn't start with that pizza, but our lives did a 180 because of it. My life has never been picture-perfect, but we got through that moment and countless others. Our struggles and our triumphs made us who we are today. I wouldn't change a thing.

What Makes the Four Steps Different

Now that you know more about me, you may understand why I developed a strategy of just four simple steps to get to financial freedom. There are some excellent programs out there that are intended to accomplish similar goals of managing your personal finances. Some are very rigid and restrictive, some are faith-based, others simply are not realistic or make assumptions that may or may not apply to your circumstances. Many of them have too many steps that can leave most of us feeling even more overwhelmed. For example, not having a credit card and never having a car payment is just a touch unrealistic for most of us; however, these are great long-term goals to set.

Mine is more of a "kitchen-table" approach. I've simplified this into a four-step plan that is a culmination of the research and work I put into my own situation:

Step One: Build an emergency fund.

Step Two: Develop a budget.

Step Three: Climb aboard the debt locomotive.

Step Four: Plan for retirement.

Over the years, I have tweaked this plan as I've assisted others. It is easy and does not require any sort of background in personal finance. At this stage, most people aren't so much in need of "wealth management" as much as simply making your paycheck work for you (instead of you just working for your paycheck).

The steps are not difficult; they are just things we have not been taught. As I mentioned, my mother is a great money manager, but it took me reaching adulthood to comprehend that. She lived on meager means and raised four children alone after my father passed, yet she was always the one in our extended family who was in a position to loan money to others when they needed it. She set a great example, but I wasn't taught things like how to balance a checkbook, or how compounding interest works. These are not things parents usually teach their children, so if these are the same sorts of things you are a little shaky on, I have got you covered.

These initial four steps led me to a point where I could do much more—and then, they propelled me to do *even more*. That does not mean they don't require some time and effort. I am asking you to be open to these four steps, and be willing to commit eighteen to twenty-four months to cleaning up, digging out, and setting yourself free. You will have the freedom that most people do not, the kind of freedom that will allow you to make even more choices toward happiness and success.

Freedom to change your job or career; freedom to work less and have more family time; freedom from financial stress and strain; freedom from whatever shame or guilt you may have been carrying. That is my hope for you, and if you're holding this book, you must be ready to change something, too. You are ready to stop living the same old way by making a change and doing something different. Even if you decide to only work through the four steps and leave it at that, your life will be very different from just about everyone else you know.

We like to think we are safe, that there will always be another paycheck, and that tomorrow is always promised to us. If the COVID pandemic taught us anything, we learned that everything isn't set in stone, like we thought it was; there are always unknowns that may be out of our control. You can find yourself on the receiving end of the financial consequences of someone else's bad behavior or problems—a virus, divorce, medical emergency, a business closing, or a job layoff.

I can remember an occasional passing thought, such as, *I really should get my finances in order...maybe I'll start next payday, or next month after we're back from vacation, or...*until I was humbled by not having enough money to order a pizza.

This book will not show you how to play the stock market or make investment decisions. If that is what you are looking for, there are plenty of books that cover wealth management. I want to help you change your mindset and get you to a place where you are not living paycheck-to-paycheck, where you are enjoying your life, and where you are no longer obsessing over financial emergencies, because now you can cover them. I want to get you to a place of Peace—with a capital P—that enables you to do all of this, and maybe order a pizza (with toppings!) every now and then.

CHAPTER 1

Why Momma's Got the Checkbook

THE MINDSET OF THE MOTHER CAN PROPEL A FAMILY UNIT INTO financial contentment. I say this upfront so that you will understand how a seventeen-year-old Chevy Montana minivan made our family rich.

My father had a heart attack while on the job at General Motors. Although he passed away at a young age, we still received his GM family discount, so Brad and I special-ordered a brand-new Chevy Montana minivan. This was our transition from a two-door car to four doors, so we got it loaded and made sure it would meet our growing family's needs. It had light-gray plush seats—perfect for capturing any spills, ground-in Cheerios, or half-eaten tacos—so I took extremely good care of that van. I had it steam-cleaned at least once a year, and every Monday morning, I cleaned out the weekend trash that our growing family had accumulated while driving to and from sports and other activities.

We loved that van. It was one of the things Brad and I had to buy, besides the house, to make room for all these kids we had. It would be twenty-five years before we purchased a brand-new car again, and we paid cash for it. My, how things have changed for us.

After the van was paid off, I took the money I had used for car payments and applied it to my retirement savings. For nearly seventeen years, we plugged those payments into our retirement accounts. No matter how well you care for a vehicle, however, it eventually starts showing its age. There were some digital things that started breaking down, and it seemed like all the repairs were $2,000 or higher. Brad and I determined we could live without the digital amenities for a while. When the automatic door stopped working, for example, we worked our biceps each time we opened and shut that heavy thing, but it was a $2,000 fix that we could live without.

I became concerned when school started back, because I dropped off a lot of kids at school in the morning. They had rules for how the kids had to get out of the vehicle for safety, and the sliding door was the only possible exit for them. They did not want the driver getting out of the car, so I couldn't get the door for them. I thought, *Should I trade in the van for something different?*

Now Josh, our youngest, was small for his age. He was born a preemie, and I'm not kidding, he stayed in size-seven jeans for three years. At the time, Sears had a return policy on Levi's where if they tore, you could get another pair the same size for free. The salesman at Sears probably thought I was getting them for other children—I am still not sure he was convinced I was truly getting the jeans for the same child each year.

I used to tell Josh, "This van is going to make us rich," so he understood my dilemma, even though he was only about seven at the time. He knew that as long as we kept that van, we had extra money, and that the extra money was not going toward the car; it was going into my retirement, and it was also going to fund our family's future.

"I'll get the door for everyone, Mom," Josh told me one day.

It was a struggle for him, but he did it. Each day, he would open that heavy door from the inside, and unload all these little kids from our neighborhood. He was the last to get out, and then he would shut it back. Even if the lady at the school offered to shut it, he would tell her, "No, trust me, you don't want to get this."

"Buddy, you're going to be the strongest kid in your class," I told him. "In fact, you may end up being the strongest kid in the world." And he would just smile, happy knowing that we were saving tons of money. Even if his friends said, "Your van's a piece of junk," which they did sometimes, he would say, "No, it's not. It's making us rich."

Usually, his reply would take them by surprise. I don't know what he said to them after that, but I could tell that the feelings that *he* had about the door were influenced by the feelings *I* had about it. If I had made a bunch of drama about it being a big inconvenience and pushed to trade it in, it might have played out differently. Instead, Josh and I would just smile at each other and think, *It is not that big of a deal.*

That is how women change the perspective for themselves and, ultimately, for their households. In spite of the many issues we had with it as it aged, I attribute my much-needed retirement boost to that van. I am going to share that retirement wealth with my kids while I'm here on this earth. I am not going to wait.

On a side note, today, Josh is a 'mini-Hulk.' He still lifts weights daily, only in the gym.

When *Should* Couples Have the Money Conversation?

It is no secret that finances are the number one reason for divorce. Many couples avoid a conversation about finances until there's a problem. And there is also the issue of how much your children should be involved in the family's finances—that fine line between teachable moments versus making them anxious and insecure.

So when *should* the subject of money come up?

Let's tackle the conversation between couples first; we will address how to handle it with children later in the chapter. Women are often reluctant to address this with someone they are dating because they think it is inappropriate and not romantic. If you are single, maybe money isn't considered a fun topic for first-date conversation, but please explore this area thoroughly before you get too serious. I am not saying it is an easy conversation, but better to start *some* conversation about finances before you are too deeply involved and can't look at things objectively.

Ideally, this subject should come up before you fall in love, because once you fall in love, I think people just go ahead down the track of going through with the marriage and thinking, *I'm going to change him*—or *I'm going to change her—from being a shopaholic*, or *from having all this debt*. So it should come up before you fall in love—but does it? Heck, no. It's not romantic. We like to put our heads in the sand, especially if we want to be married. I will admit, I didn't even think about it myself.

Some churches require couples to go through premarital counseling before they are allowed to marry, but in most cases, they are engaged and already have a date set. I think if you have reached that point, whether you attend church or not, some type of financial counseling is a good idea. Ideally, however, the subject of finances should come up before you fall in love with somebody, because that would factor into whether you are compatible. Pay attention to someone's attitude toward debt; do they mention any credit card debt, do they seem stressed, are they still living with a parent, do they never offer to pay? Even casual conversation can reveal red flags if you pay attention. Do they mention something about paying on a credit card? That opens the door to ask whether they have a lot of debt. Finances remain the top reason for divorce, and you do not want to be strapped to someone else's debt or bad spending habits if you don't have to.

By the same token, you don't have to break up with them, either. You can set a personal boundary that you will not take the relationship any deeper until they are out of debt, or have made significant strides in that area.

Quite often, if we look at how we handle our money, it can tell us just as much about us as looking in a mirror. We may discover things about ourselves that we do not like. In 2018, TD Ameritrade conducted a study that showed 41 percent of Gen X-ers and 29 percent of baby boomers ended their marriage due to disagreements about money. While the divorce rate is about 50 percent for first marriages, it's 60 percent for second marriages. We are not learning anything, apparently, between our first and second marriages. We know if we are in a state of constant worry and our finances are a mess, it influences our outlook on life.

Marriage isn't the answer to money problems and can create even more problems if money is not explored before marriage. We must get control of our finances. In fact, Pew released a report in 2010 that stated forty percent of women are single, solo breadwinners. That is a sharp increase from just 11 percent back in 1969. Among those percentages, the number of single women who have children has gone from 5 percent in 1969 to 41 percent in 2010. You can do this by yourself, and in many respects, the four steps might be easier if you are calling the shots without having to negotiate, but it can be so exhilarating to accomplish this with a partner who understands what you have done together. Likely, you would be far more selective about a partner if you have worked through the four steps and have your finances in order.

Opposites usually attract. Regardless of who controls the finances, you are capable of understanding how they work and how to fix it if they do not. Everyone in the household needs to get involved, from grandma to the five-year-old. Today's households have much different dynamics than in years past. When everyone understands what you are doing and why, everyone stays engaged.

Why Women *Should* Control the Finances

The cliché "if Momma ain't happy, ain't nobody happy" is true. Mom makes everything run in the household. She reduces mental and physical clutter. Mom is the heartbeat and the nucleus—she knows everyone's schedule, knows when it is time to pick up more milk, and her attitude sets the tone for everyone else. She knows Johnny has to be at the orthodontist by a certain time, and then straight to his ball game after that. Mom makes the family routine run smoothly, and hopefully she delegates work and tasks. She is the one making everything happen. Mom really controls the pulse and tempo of the family.

I do not want to excuse men from their responsibilities, but when it comes to finances, women come by these abilities honestly. We know how to multitask. Gary Smalley, the author and marriage counselor, explains that researchers have found that just prior to birth, large amounts of chemicals (mainly testosterone) release in the brains of baby boys, creating what researchers call "brain wash." This "brain wash" literally damages a man's ability to focus on multiple tasks at the same time and explains why men are more single-task oriented, while women are multitasked beings (they do not have that testosterone wash). That explains why men might not be able to hear her when the television is on, and why she can cook, talk on the phone, and discipline the kids at the same time. The downside of this superpower is that women tend to do too much and get over-whelmed at times.

Women determine whether the family will take a Disney vacation or take a camper to the lake. We decide if we will do a bathroom remodel, and how often we will eat at a restaurant versus firing up a grill. As author Gary Smalley says, men were made to go out and hunt, while women kind of did everything else, possibly because it took a long time to hunt. I am not undermining men, because they are an important part of the family unit, contributing to the physical, financial, and emotional health of the family, but the woman is truly made for this "Chief Financial Officer" role.

Now if you are married, you may be in a situation where your spouse considers himself the head of all things in the family, including the finances. Traditionally, men have made more money or were the only source of income. When I was growing up, that was usually the case among my friends. The church taught that men were heads of household, and many interpreted that to mean that the man did everything, and made all the decisions. If he was a smart man, however, he asked his wife for her input because he realized there were situations where they complement one another. Or perhaps they were both gifted in an area, but she was better at finances. So decisions were made together, with the family unit's best interest in mind.

What if the family believes that the man needs to handle finances? What if he is not doing it? Is he the only one to blame? Today, traditional roles are not the norm. Most families are dual income and in many cases, the wife makes as much as or more money than her spouse. We want to be equal partners and share the responsibilities. With finances, a lot of times nobody is doing anything. If you want a better life for yourself and your family, someone has to manage the money. If you are reading this, you are likely the North Star of your household.

Men also want to keep the peace. They want to please, and they want to do it quickly. I know a gentleman who was struggling financially, and he would just give his kids a hundred bucks, even if he didn't have it to give, just so they would get the heck out of the house. He wanted peace for himself, which meant he didn't want to talk about or be bothered with anything. If you are fortunate to be with a good man, and he is in charge of finances, he should also be involving you in them so that you have an idea of what is going on. Two can be better than one. What one notices, the other may miss, and vice versa.

You may be thinking, *I can change my lifestyle later. My life is so freaking stressful, I will sort this out later.* Or maybe you think you *have* tried everything and nothing works well. To that I would say, you might have tried a few things for short periods of time, and maybe they didn't work. Do you feel like you have tried a thousand things? Then I am asking you to try a thousand and one. How bad do you want it?

If Mom is happy, everybody is happy, and if you are married, your husband probably realizes this. My husband got on board and let me take the reins. He realized my passion, and he knew I was studying everything I could get my hands on. I don't mean to sound like I had a whip-and-chain sort of control over him, but we agreed to how much spending money we would receive, and he agreed to pay off debt. He also agreed to eat out less, and we went with more frequent, simple meals at home. Instead of the three-course meals we used to have, we went to meatless Mondays, taco Tuesdays, burger Wednesdays, and so on.

In 2018, TD Bank's Fourth Annual Love and Money survey estimated at least one-third of U.S. consumers identify living paycheck-to-paycheck as their top barrier to meeting financial goals. We have to do things differently, starting now. When you are on a fixed income in retirement, you don't want to depend on your kids to help out. They may likely be strapped financially themselves. I am asking you to commit to the four steps for eighteen to twenty-four months. If you put a lot of hard work into it right now, your life is going to be so much better than everyone else's. If you want something different, do something different.

'No Soda for You'

When he started seeing the benefits of taking back control of our finances, Brad helped me educate others on what to do and how to do it. He was not suffering like he thought he might, and a lot of times that is when you see real progress from the deliberate changes you have made. If you get to where you are both aligned and set on achieving the goal, it is often reached earlier. Then the blessings flow unexpectedly—maybe your tax refund is bigger, or you receive a bonus at work, or get a better job altogether. If you are a good steward, it happens. It also helps to have a united front when you bring your children into the discussion.

Earlier in the chapter, I told you I was going to address when and how to involve your kids. Unless you are preaching to them about how poor you are, your children will not know the difference beyond recognizing some changes. You do not have to tell them you can't afford things, and you know best how to word these discussions for your child. Good or bad, your attitude will have the most impact. Here are a few ideas to give you a nudge:

- Instead of a Friday night at the movies, pop some popcorn, put up a sheet in the backyard, and stream one instead.

- Instead of ordering pizza, make your own individual-size pizzas. Set up a "toppings bar" so each person can create their own.

- Instead of tickets to an amusement park, pack a simple picnic lunch and bring a frisbee, football, or even bottles of dollar-store bubbles to a local park and make some memories.

- Instead of a "credit-card Christmas" that leaves you in debt, challenge everyone to make or buy their gifts for $10 or less.

- Study up on your state's flora and fauna, then visit some state parks to see if you can locate and identify plants and animals you might come across.

- Look at when a meteor shower might be visible in your area. Take a blanket and find a good spot to watch. (Bonus if you can identify planets and constellations!)

Whatever changes you make, do it with a good attitude. The vibe should be, "This is fun. It's nice weather. Let's do it." Remember, the leader controls the pulse of the household, even if you have a "fake-it-'til-ya-make-it" attitude. Your opinions and feelings matter, and the rest of the household will follow your lead. If you are happy, everyone else will be, too.

We should teach our children about budgeting money early in their lives, if possible. It is more tolerable at an early age, but they can learn this at any age. After all, the belt-tightening is not going to be forever, because you are going to buckle down and get it in order. Whether your children receive an allowance or you give them their spending money on an as-needed basis, there are a few habits you can teach them now. When my kids were on my "payroll," they had to give some of it away. We didn't tell them they had to give 10 percent, but they had to give some, save some, and the rest they could spend if they wanted.

If we went on vacation and they wanted a souvenir, we put money in each child's envelope that they would use to buy them. I can tell you that they bought fewer trinkets when it was coming out of their own money! If they wanted a new article of clothing, they also had to select something to give away. I would take them shopping with me, so they could observe and absorb the *how* and *why* of my purchasing decisions. I mean, when you are the one pushing the cart and it's on your bill, while they are begging for everything in every aisle, you can teach them so much about math, discipline, wise choices, creative strategy—skills that will benefit them as adults.

We want to give our kids everything, but is every "thing" what is best for them? Wisdom and time spent making memories are what they really need—not the place or the cost.

My children joke about the fact that if we ate at an upscale restaurant, which we didn't do very often seeing as there are six of us, I told them they had to drink water, no soda. Same rule applied if they brought along friends. Brad's an unsweet tea kind of guy, so when I told him the rule applied to him, too, he was not game for this at all.

"You mean I'm doing this, too?"

"Yes, you have to get ice water," I replied. "If we're expecting it of them, they expect the same of us." I'm sure he quietly gave me an eyeroll or two.

My logic was that soda, running about two dollars in those days, easily added fifteen to thirty bucks to the bill, depending on how many people we had with us that day. And you are tipping based on that amount. We had a finite amount to spend each month in restaurants, and I didn't want to spend that kind of cash on soda when we had soda in the refrigerator at home. So we had a nice meal and drank water with it. When we returned home, if someone wanted a can of something, everybody's favorites were stocked in the fridge.

It was an adjustment for all of us, but a healthier choice. Honestly, there were times my kids would attempt a meltdown in the car over it. My son Logan, in particular, persisted to fight for his right to soda.

"Can I get soda this time?"

"No, nothing's changed."

"But there are free refills."

I have to admit, I admired his persistence and strategic thinking, which amounted to, "I'm going to win her over with something that's free, because she likes a good bargain."

"I don't care if there are free refills. That first one adds a lot of cost to the bill, and we're not going to do it. We're not going to waste our chunk of eating-out money on soda."

A few weeks later, after Logan's "free refills" protest, we were eating at a Mexican restaurant after church. We had the grandparents along, plus a couple of the kids' friends. Logan watched me pull eighty-eight dollars out of our restaurant envelope to pay the bill.

"Mom, there's only a twenty left in here. And it's only Sunday. Eighty-eight bucks! What does that mean?"

"That means that we probably can't even order a pizza until next Friday when I get paid, unless we take it out of grocery money."

"Well, let's not do this again." Yeah, buddy. Heard you. Loud and clear.

The restaurant markup for sodas is crazy. Alcohol's markup is outrageous. Even though my children are now adults and some have children of their own, none are big soda drinkers.

Mom is the influencer, and as a lifelong Diet Coke aficionado, I acted as though water was the absolute best thing ever (and for your health, it truly is). But when I explained to my children what we could do with the money we saved, it warmed my heart to hear them give that same reasoning to their friends later. I would overhear them say things like, "If you order a burger at Steak & Shake and just order water, you can get out of there for four bucks. Or order a chicken sandwich with a water, and it's $4.50."

Logan, especially, is so frugal now that I nudge *him* to actually spend money. When we go out to eat as a family, Brad and I still buy, and now anybody can have any drink they want—even though there are thirteen of us now. I don't have to save like I once did. And instinctively, they will turn to their kids and say, "No soda for you." That's their joke.

When it comes to bringing your children into these decisions, you can balance awareness with creativity. I think they should be made aware as early as possible, but in a calm, educating way, like helping seven-year-old Josh understand why that old van was going to make us rich. One of the worst things you can do is say something like, "We can't afford it," if they ask for a special treat or ask why you can't go on an extravagant vacation like your neighbors. Maybe you can't afford it, but why worry your child about that?

As a matter of fact, when you tell them what you are doing, try not to do it when they are begging for something. Just say *no*, and move on. Or if they pout about never getting to go anywhere for spring break, plan a few low-cost day trips and picnics, and make sure you are excited and enthusiastic about it.

Mom's attitude can do so much to make it better. That's why she has the checkbook—or should. Yes, the four steps require some small changes (and dramatic changes), but women have the power and influence to make this a positive experience for everyone. Even if you have to "fake it 'til you make it" while you are getting used to certain lifestyle changes, the rest of your household will absorb your vibe.

Abundance is not about wealth; it is about realizing you have more than enough, more than you need. And I don't think we realize that, because we see so many material things that we want. There is a light at the end of the tunnel, and we are going to find it together. Don't just learn how to earn—learn how to *live*.

WANNA HAVE FUND$?

Make an (almost) free memory. Commit to spending $20 or less and plan an outing for yourself or your family. Maybe it's a bottle of cheap wine on your back deck at sunset. Pack a lunch and buy a dollar-store kite or bubbles to spend an afternoon at a park. Visit a local museum (bonus points if it's "free admission" day!). If you have children, ask them for ideas—it's a great way to teach them about what things cost!

CHAPTER 2

Find a Plan and Stick with It

I HAVE FOUR CHILDREN, ALL FIVE YEARS APART. ASHLEY, MY OLDEST CHILD, was sixteen when my youngest child, Josh, was born. As young children, each one had a different idea about where money came from; in fact, it gave me a lightbulb moment later in life.

Ashley was with me when I was in college and very poor. I drove a Volkswagen Rabbit and it cost us about $3.40 to get back and forth from my mother's home to our college housing. Even at a young age, Ashley was aware of some of our money struggles; she would often ask me if we had enough money to get home. Occasionally, we had to tap into her piggy bank to go to our favorite pizza place, where we would share one order of breadsticks with cheese and a Coke. Ashley learned how to pay with cash and connected the dots that way.

My second child, Brandon, would ask me if I had any checks when we were in his favorite toy store. Even when he was really little, he would just say, "Do you have checks today?" He saw me paying the bills that way, and that is also how I paid for things that we wanted or needed. My third child, Logan, would ask me if we could go to the ATM; he called it the "money mover," and believed that if someone needed money, it would just spit it out. By the time Josh came along, he would always ask me if I had my debit card before we headed out to the store or if we were in a restaurant. Regardless, the boys each had a magical idea about where money comes from and, at least while they were very young, there seemed to be an endless supply of it—checks, ATMs, and debit cards held the key. They would have continued to believe this, had I not challenged them and educated them about using cash and seeing where our money went. With each of my children, spending *seemed* less painful, but was it really?

Our views on money are formed and held by old habits that we likely observed as very young children. Maybe we watched Grandma reach for the coffee can where she kept a stash of five-dollar bills, or watched Dad whip out a credit card, unaware that he also received a bill for it at the end of the month. It is the unawareness, that subconscious pattern, which can influence whether we have control of our own spending habits later in life. As you work through the four steps, pay careful attention to what you are learning and how this knowledge can teach your children or others in your circle, and perhaps break some bad cycles.

We don't want to get a debit card, push "buy now" on Amazon, or push "pay" on our favorite app and not acknowledge that they provide a buffer of sorts, making our spending decisions less painful than pulling out a pile of our hard-earned cash. Most of us do not think consciously about it, but we should. Our sweet little children need to understand that there is real money attached to these decisions. If we do not help them understand how to think differently about money, life and peer pressure will get to them like it has gotten to us. I don't think that is where most people want to end up. It is just where the wind and the times are taking them.

Recently, I read an article specifically about Gen X women and what they are dealing with right now. Their biggest worry is finances;

specifically, a large percentage have less than $50,000 saved toward retirement. Sometimes, the concern was seemingly unfounded—one woman interviewed had a million dollars in the bank, but stated she was constantly worried about money. It was really fascinating, and there were other reasons Gen X women had sleepless nights, but the underlying theme continued to be about money. When you are living paycheck-to-paycheck, even the idea of retirement seems like a pipe dream.

It bears repeating that each person's view on money and how it shapes their own plan for money should be acknowledged. Just because someone you loved did it one way does not mean you should. If you have a plan for it—to get out of debt, save, and reduce expenses—a plan puts you at the top 10 percent of society. Four steps can put you in a place of peace in eighteen to twenty-four months.

There are many good plans to choose from. Some are faith-based, some insist on a "cash-only" strategy, others focus on chipping away at debt. The problem is that most of us are just bobbing along, pulling out cards, paying through our phone apps, aimlessly, mindlessly spending without connecting that each swipe, each tap removes real dollars from our account. Then we wonder where our money goes. Trust me, the bank will remind you with a nice $40 slap across the wallet each time a transaction processes and you do not have the funds to cover it.

Most people in society do not have a plan; we just do what is being done. And what's being done is what we watched our parents and grandparents do without connecting the dots, without acknowledging that technology makes spending seem far less painful. We are doing what we're doing, and we don't even know why. That is not a legacy I wanted to pass down to my kids, and if you are reading this book, neither do you. That is why we need a plan.

You're Not Unusual, Yet

The analysis of the latest census household survey from the Center on Budget and Policy Priorities (November 11, 2020), showed that one in three adults are having trouble paying expenses. Thirty-four percent of adults reported difficulty covering basic expenses, such as food, rent or mortgage, car payments, medical expenses, and student loans. This paycheck-to-paycheck lifestyle has long been a widespread affliction.

The trouble is, of course, most of us do not work at the same full-time job or employer for forty years and retire with our gold watch, pension, and silver engraved bowl, like previous generations. Today, we switch jobs frequently and might be one missed paycheck away from financial ruin, which adds to our stress. Our vulnerabilities can be very unforgiving. Once you start down that slippery slope of debt, it is hard to climb back up before the next crisis hits.

Student loans are a particularly heavy yoke around young people. I consider these loans to be one of the biggest stealers of "the good life" that we promise so many students. Dave Ramsey has a documentary titled *Borrowed Future*, which describes student loans as the most over-looked crisis in America. Many times, I have seen college students start off with large debts right after graduation. I have seen their parents delay their own retirement because of their children's school loans. Putting the word *student* in front of *loan* makes me feel nauseated. They are only eighteen. They do not know another way. It is another example of "everyone does this," until they owe the equivalent of a house payment for fifteen years after graduation.

I have also seen medical payments and medical bills eat people alive for many years at a time. Many people, especially in large cities, can spend up to half their income on mortgage and utilities. So many people have lived this way for so long that we have normalized it. We assume this is just the way it is, because everyone is living this way.

My moment of clarity came with that pizza (or rather, the lack of funds to pay for it). I work hard. Brad works hard. Why were we working so hard but living paycheck-to-paycheck? We had swiped some new tires onto a credit card. Our kids needed soccer cleats. We needed a last-minute birthday gift for a family member. We also believed that our college degrees gave us a chance for higher-paying careers. Many of us enter the workforce with a ton of debt and, usually, entry-level jobs. We go into debt for those college degrees because we think it is going to help us.

Then, sometimes, people are cashing out their retirement savings just to stay afloat or to break even. They don't realize they are shooting themselves in the foot, repeatedly. It is going to really hurt them when they reach retirement.

Stress over money is one of the biggest causes of unhappiness. I mentioned already that it remains the number one reason couples divorce. Data from the General Social Survey (GSS) collected between 2010 and 2018 shows that married respondents are much happier and their children are more secure. If you are currently debating leaving your significant other for financial reasons, think it through. The finances may have you stressed out, but you can do something about it; you do not have to stay where you are, you do not have to break up and pay for two households. The "escape plan" of divorce isn't a very good one; in fact, I would not recommend this at all. Divorce causes financial hardship. You can go a lot further if you work with your current spouse and family to dig your way out of debt and to financial security. The end result will be priceless, and you might just end up with the relationship of your dreams. Working through difficulties is what life is about, and it makes us stronger.

Now, if you are already divorced or not currently in a relationship, this is a moot point and not meant to make you feel guilty or ashamed at all. It is what it is, and this is where you have landed. We are going to start right where you are currently. You can literally work the four steps, no matter what situation you are in.

A lot of people consider stress as a negative. In a full-blown stress response, there is a release of cortisol, the stress hormone. It usually leads to a loss of productivity, anxiety, and powerlessness. If left unchecked, it eventually causes health problems, exhaustion, and hopelessness. Stress is not always negative, however. In fact, if channeled properly, stress can be a great motivator. When we experience stress working toward a specific goal—planning a wedding, preparing for the holidays, anticipating the birth of your child—it is empowering. We have some control and feel prepared for the big event. When financial stress is redirected, you can yield the same sort of empowerment. Picking a plan is an essential step in redirecting that stress.

That is not to say that there isn't stress that comes with power, too. Even if you are budgeting and gaining control of the finances, you will feel the stress of it, but the difference is that this stress sees light at the end of the tunnel. It is that light that gives you the power. There is hope, because you have a roadmap to help you work toward a defined goal. And the pinnacle will be with the accomplishment of that goal.

That sort of power lowers the stress that you feel and can actually motivate you to do more. If you don't have a plan, though, I do not think you have a chance at the kind of power that comes with financial security. This does not happen on its own. No one gets anywhere they have not been without a road map, GPS, or a plan.

Four Essential Costs, No Matter What

There are four expenses, no matter what, that we have to pay: rent/mortgage, food, utilities, and transportation. You have to have somewhere to live. Otherwise, you will be unable to concentrate on anything else. You and your family have to have shelter from the elements. Everyone has to eat. It is a basic necessity to eat every day, from the first day of the month to the last. There is a huge difference though between steak at a fancy restaurant and rice and beans at home, but there's still a cost. Essential utilities—I'm talking temperature control and water, not internet—are things that allow us to stay clean, cook food, and stay comfortable. Transportation enables us to get to job interviews, go to work, and get to places like the grocery store or bank. Whether you use your own vehicle or a city bus, ongoing transportation is a must.

That does not mean you need to keep steak on your grocery list or purchase a new vehicle every two to four years. Regardless of your plan or strategy to reach financial health, you will need to tweak it until you have your footing on these four essentials. If your "plan" is currently just figuring out which bill does not get paid that month, then you need a *real* strategic plan so the four essentials are not at risk.

The four necessities must be paid, no matter what. I cannot emphasize this enough.

No matter your level of income, the majority of us live paycheck-to-paycheck. If you can bravely acknowledge to yourself that you are one paycheck away from trouble, you can also acknowledge how vulnerable you are. If a paycheck doesn't come in, you know your life will be in upheaval. And for some of you, you are already there. Maybe it is a sudden job loss, or a slow drip because of reduced hours, or you have been hit with an unexpected bill from a medical emergency or appliance repair. Regardless of whether you acknowledge you are vulnerable or you are already there, if you would talk about it among your friends, they are likely in similar positions. This reinforces how much we have normalized financial insecurity, and many of us have accepted this as the norm. When *every* dollar coming in is also going out, consumption is controlling your life!

Sadly, it is an unpleasant financial reality for most Americans. According to a 2016 Bankrate survey, 69 percent of Americans have less than a thousand dollars in savings. And nearly 80 percent of American workers say they are living paycheck-to-paycheck. A 2017 report from CareerBuilder.com showed that women are particularly vulnerable, with

81 percent having reported living this way (compared to 75 percent of men). The average car payment is $500 or more per month, and in some households, their cell phone bill also comes close to that.

I am not trying to shame anyone here. Things happen. Life happens. So much is out of our control. Believe me, I know what this feels like, and I operated the same way for many years. Why do we accept these terms? Living paycheck-to-paycheck does not have to be the norm, and there is another way to live that offers peace and contentment.

Quick Action for a Different Normal

When day-to-day emergencies could throw you over the edge, you know it is time for a change. If you want to change this situation, I have a way for you to do it. And just because everyone else lives this way does not mean you or your family has to live this way. There are ways to avoid this pit and the stress marks that it leaves on your life. The essentials are home, food, utilities, and transportation. Beyond that, there are a number of plans to find your financial footing. The only outstanding issue is whether you are willing to forgo some immediate pleasures to take that stress off your back.

There are many plans out there. The trick is picking one and sticking to it. My plan consists of four simple steps. When you are just starting on this particular road to recovery, four steps seems much more manageable and achievable.

I've already stated that I am a firm believer in "quick action," so I am going to provide you with some quick starting points. We will take a much deeper dive into budgeting and debt in later chapters, but there are a lot of practical things you can do right now to jumpstart the process. Let's start with your recurring bills.

Ask yourself:

- Can this bill be lowered by calling the company and setting up a reasonable payment plan?

- Can we get by (for eighteen to twenty-four months) with a smaller plan—or no plan—for our cell, internet, or TV (remember, those are not essential utilities)?

- Can we issue a "spending moratorium" on certain items, like specialty coffee or fountain drinks, for eighteen to twenty-four months?

- Can we make our own lunch(es) instead of buying it?

- Can we walk instead of drive?

- Can we set the thermostat lower in the winter and higher in the summer, and bundle up or run a fan when needed?

If you take just a few minutes to think about little things that you can do right now, you might see immediate extra money in your account each month that can help you work this plan. Baby steps are still steps in the right direction, and the results should motivate you to do more. A written, scalable plan is your best (and next) move.

My four-step model includes a financial plan. Why do plans work? If you follow a plan, it will work to get you debt-free and financially stable. You just have to apply what you learn. Why do budgets work? Because budgets help you avoid spending more than you earn. If you know what your income is and know what you are spending, you can adjust the spending and make sure that you are living within your income.

One couple that I counseled was spending $700 a month eating out, and they were not contributing anything into retirement. They were middle-aged, but on the younger side of middle age, and they both worked hard. I do not want to use the word "entitled," but they felt just like I did that night with the pizza; they were tired after working all day. Why shouldn't they be able to enjoy a nice meal prepared by someone else? But I asked them to write down what they spent and to be honest. When they realized just how much they were spending on dining out, they decided that the meals taste good, and they still don't like cooking, but not to the tune of $700 a month when nothing is being put toward retirement.

We will get into how budgets actually give you greater flexibility and less restriction later on, but for now, I want you to agree to give it time, because finding financial freedom does not happen overnight. You did not get in the situation you are in overnight, so don't expect to get out of it any quicker. And guess what? Things are still going to happen. Life is still going to happen. Unexpecteds do not go on vacay just because you have decided to get on a plan that will get your finances in order. So don't just try this for six months then say it did not work. As I have been saying, it takes eighteen to twenty-four months to see real results.

You will need to give it that time, reassess it, and readjust it before you just abandon it. If you are not getting the desired results, or you are suddenly hit with a major expense, tweak your plan. In fact, my plan was gleaned from a number of plans and strategies I had studied. I read through one that wanted me to pay off my house. Another instructed me to start paying on my children's 529 plans and college funds. There were others who advised me to focus on this, focus on that, and it was all good advice. The question was, where did these fit for me on the priority scale?

I entered my marriage to Brad with two kids in tow. I also wanted my house paid off, so that was my priority. I decided I would figure out how to send my children to college later. Brad and I agreed that we would help them as much as we could, but paying off our home was the priority. We had it paid off by the time my third child entered college, so we funneled what had been our house payment into college expenses after that.

Credit Cards as a Backup?

Other plans will instruct you to shred your credit cards, freeze them in blocks of ice, or anything else to get them out of your hands. They argue that cash is painful and, therefore, it is necessary to pay everything with actual, cold hard cash, so you feel it. I agree with the sentiment behind these ideas, but for me, it did not work. It was unrealistic for me to pay cash for everything, though I decided to do it for expenses that could vary a lot, like groceries and eating out. I also do not like keeping track of multiple debits when I balance my checkbook. I feel a credit card is safer against theft, but your goal should be to use it only for needs, and to pay it off each month to avoid interest charges. If you can't do this, get rid of them!

I do not use my credit card for consumables. I travel a lot with my job, however, and hotel reservations often require a credit card. We use a gas card that we pay off each month, because there are rewards and extra benefits we receive from it that are quite lucrative. In fact, we roll the fifty to one hundred dollars that we get in quarterly rewards back into the gas payment.

We are going to attack spending and debt, I can assure you, but you do not have to get rid of credit cards altogether, unless that is your biggest problem. I will admit, for a while, this was a big problem for me. I said over and over that I was going to pay it off every month, and even when I did get on track a few times, I would derail and end up with a big balance on my credit card. Keeping one or very few cards is also a good idea.

A more manageable goal is to learn to use credit cards responsibly and, for eighteen to twenty-four months, try your hardest not to use them at all. Give yourself a chance to learn how they work and what it means to be responsible with your credit. If you can't make this adjustment, or recognize that your credit card is a major point of weakness in your plan, shift to a debit card and don't use the credit card at all. So for now, if you are using a credit card, don't charge more than you can pay each month, and really try not to use it at all for the next several months.

Another reason to hang on to your credit card is your credit score. Monitor your balances closely, because available credit factors into your credit score. Regardless of what some financial teachers might tell us, most of us need a credit score to buy a house or any type of a car. Ideally, it is recommended that we use less than 30 percent of the credit available on any type of credit account, including credit cards. So if a company extends $5,000 credit to you, never carry more than a $1,500 balance. And for now, don't worry if you owe more than 30 percent on any of it; we will tackle debt here shortly.

What about big things, like back-to-school shopping or vacation? At this stage, I would say proceed with caution. As a mother of four, I know how expensive even the most basic back-to-school items can be. Reward cards make things super-tempting when you are on vacation, or just want something. They will not delay school just for you to get caught up on your finances. Proceed with caution here. Do stay-cations or day trips and the minimal essentials for back to school. You can revisit what you need in one month.

Remember the small, quick-action steps I listed earlier in the chapter? If you are facing large expenses but haven't incurred them yet, take a moment to see if there are alternatives so the expense is not quite so brutal:

- If your school requires uniforms, is there a way to purchase them used, or more cheaply?

- If there is an item your child will need for a specific class, like an instrument or expensive equipment, can you look into renting or check out consignment shops?

- If you want to get away, could you borrow some camping equipment and set out on a local adventure? Or, if you had a specific destination in mind, is there camping nearby?

- Could you take a series of day trips and buy tickets to area attractions for vacations?

- Could you buy your college school books on Amazon, or another online book market—and buy them used, if possible?

Much like your daily spending habits, commit to a series of baby steps to wean you off using a credit card until you become better acquainted with interest rates, promotional rates, late fees, annual fees, and all the rest. If you truly struggle with taking a break from your credit card, you need to communicate promptly with the card issuer and work with them to get on a reasonable payment plan, while coming to terms with not having a credit card at all.

The Big Secret to Financial Security

Finally, I have read through numerous financial plans, and most of them offer a lot of good ideas, they really do. The main problem is that most people do not choose one. They get overwhelmed by their day-to-day living expenses and feel like the plan's author doesn't understand them or could not possibly identify with their specific circumstances. It does not matter which one you choose—my plan or someone else's—I just want you to leave the paycheck-to-paycheck mentality behind, permanently, and get to a better place.

The only "big secret" to get you there is to find a plan and stick with it. Understand that no plan is a "one-size-fits-all," but do seek the one that fits with what you know about yourself and your spending habits.

Know that you will likely have to tweak the plan from time to time, and it does not mean you are a failure; it means you are working the plan for your situation and living your life.

I mean, think about it. Aren't you tired yet? Aren't you tired of looking at your account and saying, "I hope I make it to the next paycheck"? If that is not where you want to be, you have to do what you have never done. This is something you should contemplate. Just in case you missed it the first time: *if you do not like where you are, change it.*

Strive to get to the point where every big-ticket item, major expense, and emergency does not require a credit card. Stay tuned for Step One of my financial plan.

WANNA HAVE FUND$?

Since I am challenging you to make a change, here's one that's *not* money-related. Think about a route you take on a regular basis—to work, to church, to book club—and take a different route, or take a different mode of transportation. Is the destination within a mile? Walk to it. Is it across town and you have to pay to park? Take the city bus. Take a look around—what have you missed by taking the same route each day? What have you discovered? Does this change awaken your senses and make you more alert? If you can change your path to work, think about how you can change your path financially.

CHAPTER 3

Step One: Create an Emergency Fund

REMEMBER GRANDMA? IT SEEMS LIKE SHE ALWAYS HAD A "CASH-STASH" for emergencies. Coffee cans, jewelry boxes, nightstands, an empty shoe box in the top of a closet. Grandma could get her hands on money quickly, if necessary. I loved both of my grandmothers, and I remember exactly where they kept their stashes.

Grandma's emergency stash was usually earmarked for things like fixing Grandpa's broken truck. Other times, it was for ice cream and a movie—not exactly an emergency, but it didn't exactly wreck the cash-stash, either. This became a thing of the past around 1946, when credit started emerging and charge cards surfaced. At first, these amenities were only available to a few people who had money and were doing business with specific merchants. But by the 1950s, credit cards became more readily available to everyone.

Then revolving credit started, which allowed cardholders the convenience of not having to pay off their credit card balance each month. When they had emergencies, they could reach for plastic and pay it off over time, even though they had to pay extra in interest.

It does not take long for the collective debt to pile up, because there are numerous "emergencies" of varying degrees every month. We push out the payments further and further, and more "emergencies" arrive before we pay the others off, until our most basic needs can only be met, sometimes, with a credit card. Yikes. How did we get here?

Most would agree that these "emergencies" always come at the wrong time. Why do they always have lousy timing? Because no one wants to plan for these expenses, and most of us are usually not prepared financially to take care of them.

When I think back to my mother, she has always been able to manage the money. Even when my father died at the young age of 44, she somehow became the one who people came to when they had a financial crisis and needed to borrow money. I suspect she was also the one who made the *least* amount of money—she just knew how to manage it very, very well. I remember she always paid off her credit card bill each month. She shopped at garage sales. She found less expensive ways to purchase what we needed and wanted. Having grown up dirt poor, she managed to learn these skills.

Alas, I did not get her knack for money management through osmosis or genetics. Neither did my children—not at first, anyway. My mother was the best mother and father role model we could have ever asked for, but I did not absorb her talent for money management. I had to learn it on my own through trial and error. We have more money and more options for credit these days, which complicates the learning process.

Fast forwarding to pre-"pizza night": So many times our family of six would decide we were going to get rid of some of our debt. We would start a plan, work at it for a while, then drop back into our old spending habits. And the debt spun madly on. When Christmas or the family vacation rolled around, we would find ourselves digging out of the hole again six months later, until the next big expense came, only to do the same thing over and over again. As a scientist (I'm a nurse practitioner), shouldn't I know that if I do the same thing over and over again, I should not expect different results?

There are many potential unexpected expenses every month, maybe every day. Unless we have an emergency fund (Grandma's cash-stash), we are always going to be reaching for the plastic, or some other way of financing our expenses.

A New Bedroom Set Is *Not* an Emergency

What is an emergency fund? It's a pool of liquid—meaning actual, real—money set aside for unforeseen expenses, like a car repair or a medical bill. An emergency fund ensures we have life's unexpected expenses covered. Having a robust emergency fund gives you some peace of mind. None of us really want to live paycheck-to-paycheck. Even though we say everybody is living this way, do you really want to be unable to pay the rent, or be just one car breakdown away from not being able to get to work? An emergency fund gives you some freedom.

Now, before your eyes glaze over on this concept, I want to take a moment to make a few distinctions between big expenses, unexpecteds, and emergencies, because it is important you understand the differences so that this fund is built—and used—wisely.

We already know from Chapter 2 what the four necessary living expenses are: rent/mortgage, utilities, food, and transportation. Those are usually what we consider to be the necessities of life.

Big expenses are those things that we want to save up for, or we know we are going to need again, which might be a newer car, a new couch, a love seat, a new bedroom set, holidays, travel, you get the idea. None of these fall into the category of "emergencies and unexpecteds."

So what are the emergencies that should be covered by your fund? Emergencies are those situations that affect your ability to pay for the four necessities of life. Your emergency could be medical, broken appliances (major appliances, not your fancy slow cooker or air fryer), a malfunctioning furnace or air conditioner, or vehicle repairs.

According to a 2019 study published by Lorie Konish on the CNBC website, academic researchers found that 66.5 percent of all bankruptcies were tied to medical issues—either because of high costs for care, or time away from work. Their research found an estimated 530,000 families turn to bankruptcy each year because of medical issues and bills. I recommend that your emergency fund be robust enough to also cover your insurance deductible, just in case. An emergency is not a new $600 purse that you bought because you had a bad day—retail therapy is not an emergency.

In 2013, the Federal Reserve Board conducted a survey to "monitor" the financial and economic status of American consumers. They asked these respondents, *How would you pay for a $400 emergency?* Forty-seven percent said either they wouldn't be able to cover the expense, or they would only be able to cover it by selling something or borrowing the money. Or, worst case scenario, they would not be able to come up with the money at all. It is only four hundred bucks; this is astonishing. Who knew?

That is only the 47 percent who were willing to respond to that particular question. For many, financial problems are a source of shame that they would rather not reveal or even discuss on any given day.

A sizable majority of Americans are on thin ice, financially. A 2014 Bankrate survey found:

- Only 38 percent of Americans could cover a $1,000 emergency room visit or a $500 car repair through money they had saved. When you consider that most ER visits and car repairs exceed those amounts, they are going to be financing it one way or another.

- Fifty-five percent of households do not have enough liquid savings (cash on hand) to replace even one month's income.

- Seventy-one percent are concerned about having enough money to cover everyday expenses.

A 2014 survey from the American Psychological Association revealed that 54 percent of Americans admitted they had "just enough" or not enough each month to meet their expenses. They found this to be our country's number one stressor. What does it mean if you don't have enough to cover basic expenses?

- You cannot afford to live a healthy lifestyle, which sets the stage for disease.

- You are so financially strapped, you do not schedule doctor's visits or wellness checkups (or at least, don't go as often as you need to).

- You do not take prescribed medications because you think "I feel okay" or that it doesn't help, and therefore you don't want to spend the money.

- You do not really have plans of going back to the doctor, because you can't take his/her advice of eating a healthier diet that costs more, or exercising when you are just worn out because of worry and stress.

It is a daily humiliation, and even a form of social suicide, because while you might be willing to tell someone you are sick, or that you've got some other type of struggle going on, you are less likely to tell someone that you can't afford four hundred bucks to pay for something. Silence is your only protection.

Even though they might need help, a good many people do not share what is going on with their finances; instead, they hide it. They have no plan, which means they do not see any light or hope at the end of the tunnel. It is not happening just to the poorest among us; it is happening to middle-class professionals, and even the upper-class whose gross income is well into the six figures and beyond. Financial insecurity has no generational boundaries, either—it is happening to the soon-to-be retired, new college graduates, high school dropouts, retirees, we are all in it, all over the country.

So why are emergencies and unexpecteds seemingly so insurmountable? In part, because we do not think they will happen to us, and when they do, we are not prepared. They are not fun expenses, like Christmas or vacations. Let me be clear: I can't force your hand on this, but an emergency fund is not intended to be spent on big-ticket items like a new car or couch. If you use your emergency fund to buy a couch, what happens when your child breaks an arm and you owe a thousand bucks in medical expenses?

If you really want to know why there is such deep economic discontent in America today, it is because a lot of people can't get ahead. It is usually because they have no plan. Yes, things are expensive, but we still have no plan. When people get some money, like a bonus, a tax refund, or maybe a small inheritance, they are more likely to spend it than to save it. They feel like they "deserve to have something," because they work hard, and yet they are unable to get ahead.

We are going to have funds designated for big expenses, I promise you, but they are not part of the emergency fund. I know it is tempting. You have worked hard to get a couple thousand dollars into an account, and it feels like it is just sitting there, while you eat a meal of beans and rice. Yes, you deserve to have something—you deserve to have peace and financial stability. Exhale. Give me eighteen to twenty-four months. Beans and rice are not forever, as you will see.

Where to Stash the Cash

Remember in the last chapter, where we talked about the stress of money? That is why we need emergency cash. Right here is where you need to think, *What would Grandma do?* First, figure out where to stash your cash.

I do not recommend that you stash it in, for example, a CD, because you would be penalized if you needed to withdraw it. I recommend a savings or money market account where it might earn less interest, but it will be accessible when you need it.

We know that financial insecurity is associated with depression, anxiety, and loss of personal control that leads to marital difficulties. We have already said that it keeps you up at night and makes you not want to get up in the morning. It forces you to just seclude yourself from the world. It affects your sense of self-worth, self-confidence, energy, and, worst of all, your hope. The sad thing is that it is largely hidden from public view. We suffer in silence.

Collectively, it also seems to have diminished our national spirit. A *New York Times* 2014 poll found that only 64 percent of Americans said they believe in the American Dream—that's the lowest figure in two decades. We need to feel that we are advancing in the world, and we want to feel that our kids are going to be able to go beyond our own accomplishments.

Just one unexpected bill is what separates millions of Americans from financial disaster. Most people in the U.S. feel depressed, with people in the lowest income brackets facing the biggest challenges, because they do not have enough money for basic needs, like food. Many families walk this tightrope with little to no savings, and you can hardly blame the pandemic, since these statistics were gathered before 2020. They are worse since the pandemic, though.

If you find yourself in any of the above percentages, what should be the initial goal when you start an emergency fund? While it would be nice to have a goal of four months of expenses, that is not realistic for the person living paycheck-to-paycheck.

Set a goal of somewhere between $1,000 to $2,000, depending on whether you have a family or you are single, and whether you rent or own your home. Most major emergencies—including insurance deductibles—fall somewhere within this dollar amount, and you will still have a bit leftover if you have to dip into it. And if you do have to dip into it, reset the clock and replenish it, with the same goal of $1,000 to $2,000.

Back to my original question: where to stash the cash? We've talked about the risk of putting it in a CD and suddenly needing the cash before its maturation date. And yes, I realize that there is not much interest earned in a savings or money market account. However, this plan is still better than leaving it in your checking account, because you really won't earn any interest there. People are also more likely to debit and dip into their checking account. It will diminish by the nickel-and-dime method of spending. Obviously, you would want to read the finer details on each type of account, but savings and money market funds keep things liquid and there is no penalty if you take it out. You need to keep it somewhere where it is easy to access for an emergency. So if Grandma's old coffee can stash keeps you on the straight and narrow with your emergency fund, then use it!

Wait—what? What do I mean by keeping you on the "straight and narrow"? Look, this isn't mad money, glad money, or sad money. You are going to use it solely for emergencies when you absolutely have to tap into it. Then you are going to replenish it. If the temptation is there to tap into it, even just a little, maybe you should keep the fund in a different account or maybe even at a different bank than what you use to pay your bills. Your emergency fund is like an insurance policy, and once you have it, you should guard it carefully. It's not a piggy bank, so do not use it for incidental expenses. Remember, it always takes much longer than anticipated to replenish it, so you do not really want to spend it if you can help it.

We will revisit the emergency fund when we get into the chapters on budgeting and debt, but for now, understand that before you pay any extra on your bills, you are going to replenish that emergency fund. Why? Because there will be another emergency at some point.

Where Is the Cash to Build and Replenish?

So where do you find the cash to build and replenish your emergency fund? Where is it hiding? A lot of people sell things or work to make extra money. You may have basic expenses met with the money coming in currently, and you might consider cutting out things like cable television, but that is not quick money. You will not benefit until the following month on that kind of stuff.

It is best if you do something that is quick—but I do want to discourage you from loans of any kind, even from a nice relative. You have not proven that you are very good with finances, and owing money to a family member is something that can make Thanksgiving dinner taste terrible and feel uncomfortable.

Eventually, you are going to find this cash when we get your budget in line. In the meantime, here are a few additional ways you can get your hands on some replenishing funds:

- Sell things—sell a lot of things via social media and websites.

- Have a garage sale.

- Sell one big-ticket item, like an extra vehicle or boat.

- Get a part-time or seasonal job until you can replenish your emergency fund.

- If you can't get a part-time job because it would cost you more for babysitting and gas, learn to make things that can be sold, such as knitting, monogramming, or other crafts.

- Babysit for others.

- Drive for a service, like food delivery or rideshares.

- Get a roommate or rent a room in your home.

- Refinance your mortgage.

- Ask for a raise.

Remember, this is temporary, and you may also find something that is fulfilling and could even lead to a promotion or a job change.

If you do not have extra time to make more money, you are going to have to find ways to spend less by cutting some expenses. Cutting or decreasing expenses will propel you to the finish line much more quickly! If you can make extra money and cut expenses, your debt will erase much faster. This can be a big step in developing your budget, which is Step Two in my financial plan. Start by writing out what you spend. Some of what you will see is obvious. Cut out the frivolous spending first (at least temporarily). Many of us spend way too much money on food and beverages—groceries, fancy coffee drinks, alcohol, takeout, restaurants—and almost everyone can cut down on this category.

Next, do a little comparison shopping on your insurance and credit card rates. You would be amazed at the deals and discounts you can get if you're willing to spend a little time doing some research. You can go to einsurance.com and compare home, life, health, and car insurance rates. If your credit is good, look into a zero-interest credit card; some of them offer twelve months zero interest, which will also help you pay down debt. If you change television and internet services, or cut the cord on television altogether, just temporarily, this can save you a lot of money.

There are many ways you can approach this, but I want you to try to build and replenish your emergency fund as fast as you can. Some people I have taught were able to scrape together $200–$500 more to add to the emergency fund when they got rid of the fees from multiple accounts and consolidated those accounts.

So how much should we strive to have at all times in that emergency fund? And how often should we revisit our emergency fund goals? Right now, strive to maintain somewhere between $1,000 to $2,000 at all times, and revisit this in another three to six months. If you can get to that first $1,000 threshold right now, you are doing great and you can get started on your plan.

What if it has been three months, and you haven't touched your emergency fund? That's great, and hang tight, because you want to make sure you have something in it at all times. Do not think of ways to spend it.

When the Emergency Exceeds the Emergency Fund

If your emergency exceeds the fund you earmarked to pay for it, go ahead and use the fund to pay toward it. The balance, unfortunately, will need to be financed, put on a credit card, or some other means. Let's say your HVAC dies a sudden death. You have got to have heating and cooling (unless it's that fortunate time of year when you can open windows). Use the emergency fund for a down payment and then pay only the minimum required for all other debt payments to build your emergency fund back up, including the HVAC payments. Once the emergency fund has been replenished, you will start hitting the debt again.

By now, you may be thinking, "Can't I catch my breath, even once? I've finally got two grand in my emergency fund. Can I take a breather and celebrate this milestone?" And to that, I will say that some people work better on a rewards system. Can you loosen the purse strings without ripping it wide open? Celebrate with a nice meal at a restaurant, and let that be it? Or maybe it is one piece of costume jewelry, a new fishing lure, or a favorite dessert? Fine. Select one and be done. The question is, how fast do you want to meet your goals? Massive action and discipline will get you to your goals more quickly, but if you are the type of person that operates on a reward, make it a small reward that is accessible to you, and get back at the quick action you are taking to get your finances in order.

Regardless, we are going to put a pin in the emergency fund once you reach $2,000. We will come back to it in a few months, and later on, we will build it up even more. For now, rest easy that you have socked away $2,000, and the next time the refrigerator stops working or your child needs stitches, you have a way to cover the cost.

We are about to dig much deeper in Step Two to find other ways to cover even more costs. Buckle up—we are just getting started!

WANNA HAVE FUND$?

Find one frivolous expense and do without it for sixty days. Put the money you'd normally spend in a jar and see how much you've saved. Based on that amount, calculate what you might spend in a year and decide whether you should resume the expense or kick it to the curb. Put the money from the jar into your emergency fund.

CHAPTER 4

Step Two: I Know, Budgets Are Scary

BRADY AND SANDRA (NOT THEIR REAL NAMES) WERE STRESSED OUT. Their tight expressions told me everything I needed to know about their relationship, but they provided me with the finer details anyway. They were headed for divorce and had come to me to help them sort out their finances so they could start the proceedings. One item they were united on, however, was that neither wanted to make a budget.

Both knew that their "budget"—using that term loosely—was not working well for either one of them. They were totally stressed, and they wanted to get their finances squared away so they could move forward separately. Most of their issues revolved around spending, and neither could live with the other's spending habits.

In fact, both were spenders, and each was upset with the other because they just knew it was the other one's fault. Their attitude was,

"I'm gonna do whatever I want, because he/she is doing whatever they want." Ultimately, it was Sandra who suggested they work together, and work with me, to get their finances in order before she took their daughter and moved out.

Brady agreed to this idea because he just wanted out; he admitted he had lost all love in the relationship. If that were true, I am not sure they would have bickered as much as they did. You could hardly call either one of them indifferent about the other, that's for sure.

When we got to this step in their process, Brady looked at Sandra angrily and said, "Say good-bye to your shoe shopping."

"Well, say good-bye to golfing and upgrading your clubs," Sandra replied, with anger and hurt. Turning to me, she said, "Let's just forget this. There is no hope for us." They left my office. Clearly, they each remembered how to push each other's buttons with the shoes and golf clubs.

Now you may be thinking, *What's the big deal? Shoes don't cost* that *much*. Well, some of them do, and if you own 150 pairs, it doesn't matter if they cost ten dollars or ten thousand dollars, they are not going to get you to retirement. Brady and Sandra were playing chicken with each other so they could call it quits on creating a workable budget. As they undercut one another, they could reinforce that the love had been lost between them. I sensed Sandra still loved Brady, but Brady's feelings were not quite as obvious. Regardless, they both had fear, knew each other's weaknesses, and knew how to use them against the other person. Every time they talked about making changes, the conversation was always about how "you" were going to change, not "I" or "we." Sandra would say, "You're going to have to do this." Brady would reply, "Well, you're going to have to do *this*." The bottom line, it was just scary for both of them.

This is one way a lot of people stay immobilized from creating a budget. They worry that they will not get to spend money on anything fun, even if it is just going out to lunch or some other simple pleasure.

This was, in a manner of speaking, Brady and Sandra's "pizza moment." You know, the "I work hard for my money, and if I want new curtains or if I want to get my kids the latest shoes, I should be able to do it." So you shift blame to the other adult, using their weaknesses against them. You stay immobilized, which really is not what either person wants. They just need help moving forward from here.

About a month later, Brady and Sandra called me. "We have to come up with a budget," they explained. "Because right now, we can't even afford to hire a lawyer." Well, if divorce is the main motivator, at least for now, so be it.

When we sat down and worked on their budget, I realized that both of them made good money. Enough that each could have some "blow money," for fun spending. As soon as I pointed this out to them, their expressions changed; they softened, and there was less tension in the air. While neither would get as much as they would like, there was shoe money and golf-club money that could accumulate over the next six months while they paid off some of their debt. After we set up their budget, and once they got through knocking out some of their debt, they could increase those two funds if they wanted.

Despite both of them being totally stressed, and knowing that what they were doing just compounded the stress, they had been charging whatever "wants" they had to pacify whatever pain they were experiencing. Both agreed to receive the same amount per fund; so if one received $100 that month, the other received it, too. It worked out well, once they realized that developing a budget—and sticking to it—for two years did not mean they couldn't have any fun. Almost immediately, those tight expressions melted into something more peaceful, and it was really priceless to see them. They just seemed so relieved.

What happened next should not have been surprising. They both became super-motivated to get moving on the budget so they could end their marriage, and it ended up saving their marriage instead. So see? Money management *can* have a romantic side!

Now, if you are single and thinking the moral to the story is that you only need a budget to save your marriage, hold tight—you are not off the hook. In fact, you have the opportunity to get it right before deciding whether you will share your life with someone else. Many single people feel the exact same way that Brady and Sandra did. They do not know how to stop doing what they're doing. And they are scared that they're not going to get anything they want, even though they work hard.

All told, budgets are scary because it is the fear of the unknown. If you have never set up a budget or have never stuck to one, part of what is steeped in that fear is that as hard as one works, you fear there will not be anything left for what you want. People hear the word *budget* and immediately think in terms of restrictive, binding, no fun. When we were younger, we thought we were going to keep all of our earnings. We thought, *When I get a job, I'm going to do whatever I want with my money. It's going to be so cool.* Then we find out that plan does not work, because we owe the money to everyone else. All of our money gets sucked out for bills and payments.

So I think we can agree that the word *budget* scares a lot of people. They think it means that they can't buy new curtains for their living room. They will never get another vehicle. They will not be able to afford Christmas this year. A lot of people overspend at holiday time, and it sets them up for trouble the rest of the year. The truth is, *budget* means the exact opposite. You can now afford what you need and pay for it in peace, with a capital P.

Tell It Where to Go

Developing a budget is, essentially, just telling your money where to go. You are going to spend the money anyway, so why not know where it is going? You do not develop a budget one night, and start using it the next. If you are new to this, understand that the process of developing a workable budget may take a few months.

You see, when you pick a plan and develop a budget, then you can make a conscious choice. *Do I want $700 a month going here? Or there? Or would I like to have something for retirement later?* Prioritizing and making decisions will help you plan for the future more effectively. If you have a plan, it makes it easier to figure out how much you think is going where and if you can save anything. You can assess if you really want to spend that much in that way.

With a plan and a budget, you also have greater financial freedom. Many people will not develop a budget, and they hate the word because they think it is going to be restrictive. The truth is, budgets give you greater flexibility. You have enough money to live on until the next payday. You save money, escape debt, and channel your funds toward things that you really care about.

Look, you picked up this book because you have an idea that you are fairly vulnerable right now. You are financially fragile; regardless of how you got there, acknowledgment of this is a big step forward, and nothing to be ashamed of (please don't ever let someone shame you for this when most of our nation is in the same boat).

So now that you have taken this big step, we have to make sure that the budget is realistic, because a good budget will allow you to live in a way that is comfortable and reasonable enough that you will actually stick to it. That is not to say it won't be tweaked a few times, especially in the beginning, but you have got to stay on top of it. You will discover things you had not realized you'd been spending so much money on, or see how you forgot about certain expenses that need to be factored in. Then you can make decisions.

I am going to level with you. Developing a plan and selecting a budget will not work unless you say *no* to some things in life. You will need to exercise a little bit of self-control to avoid the unnecessary spending and put it toward what matters most to you. Here are the three general steps you will take to develop your budget, and we will take a deeper look at each one:

1. **Start by writing down everything that you spend, every day.** It is going to take a couple of months to know what you are spending, but when you figure this out, you can make some choices. This does not mean you shouldn't start the budget yet, just understand that it might need correction. The problem is really that most of us do not know where we are spending money, because we don't keep track of it. For now, do not be hung up on *where* you are spending it, just write it down without judgment.

2. **Take ownership of what has been done, and lean into what you are about to do.** I was sick and tired of not having extra money. I wanted to order pizza on that Wednesday night instead of cooking, and I would have to take money out of our tiny savings account to do it. I knew there had to be a better way. I also had to own where I was in the present, and commit to making necessary changes to not reside there any longer. You have arrived at the same place. Maybe you have been counting dimes to pay for a latte instead of a pizza, but you have realized there has to be a better way. (Spoiler alert: There is, and we are learning it!)

3. **Make informed choices about your spending.** Look, if you want to spend $700 a month eating at fabulous restaurants, that is totally up to you. What I care about is that you are aware of the *amount* being spent, and *where or how* it is being spent. If you didn't know this before, you will know it once you review everything you have written down. You can decide if you want to continue that, or tell a portion of that money to go elsewhere,

funneling some of it to other areas that are more important to you. If you delegate money from your income each month into specific areas, you are going to be able to buy what you need in those areas.

When we bought our house, we wondered if we could afford the payment. Everywhere we turned, lenders were telling us we could. Since we had only been renters, we did not know that they were not considering our children's school tuition and other expenses into what house payment we could afford. Turns out we couldn't afford it at all, so we had to refinance, which also costs money. Our problem was getting a 15-year mortgage instead of a 30-year, but a real question might be if you can afford the item at all. Many put furniture payments (we did), credit card payments, and car payments into this same category, and it will mess up you and your budget! It is not a question of whether you can afford the payments; that is like a house of cards, and it is going to fall. We cannot base our bills on just affording the payments.

It does not have to be like this. You do not have to live like everyone else and have that stress all the time. It takes the joy out of life. Most people can get out of debt and feel relief in eighteen to twenty-four months. Would you like some peace? Yes, please. Make mine a double, in fact.

The Root Cause of Financial Bondage (and Why You Shouldn't Trust the Gas Pump to Gauge Yours)

I want to take a slight detour here, only because I think it will help you understand why a budget is essential to financial freedom. We are in the shape that we're in because financial bondage exists when there is an excess of debt, or a misuse of the money, compared to your income.

Yes, this can result from a *lack* of money, but mostly it is the result of overspending. It is common in today's culture where wants have become necessities. Our cell phones and the different plans available to us can add up to what our parents spent on their mortgage.

It is true that some families have enough money to be undisciplined and get away with it, financially speaking, but true financial freedom requires that we be good stewards. This requires action and discipline in order to make it work. Those two words do not sound fun, I know, and they may require some sacrifice (another word that is not fun).

We live in a "microwave society" where we want everything *now* and we use credit to attain it. We do not *have* to get what we want now, and usually when we do, it brings us only fleeting happiness. The stress of paying for it stays around much longer, because eventually, it seeps into the ability to get what we actually *need*. New things only smell new for a little while, but the big payment stays around much longer!

In case you missed it: wants and needs are two different things. A budget will not prohibit your fun, but it may delay certain aspects of it. You will have money going into all categories, including recreation, fun, and blow money. This allows you some flexibility in terms of how it will be spent. Will you spend it now, or each month? Or will you decide to up your game and save up for some "big fun" in the future? That is entirely up to you. The good news is that you will have fun money without the stress of it following you home by way of a credit card statement.

Trust me, meals paid with budgeted fun money taste so much better than meals paid for by a credit card. And guess what? Movies are more fun and vacations are more relaxing when paid for with money that was budgeted for the occasion. Yes, "big fun" usually requires contributing and saving for it—but it also maximizes that fun with the peace of mind that you have got it covered. Remember when I talked about "being present"? You can be fully present for the memories you are making instead of worrying about how long it will take you to pay something off.

When I am working with someone and we get to the budget step, I am often asked how they can trim the fat on their spending. I do not necessarily want someone to feel like they have to give up their lattes, or go into hyper-restrictive mode, because they will not stay there very long (trust me on this). The other side of that coin is that if you can cut back completely and wait it out, you will achieve your financial goals faster. Know that this is only temporary. Hear me on this: if you tighten the belt too much, you will cut off the "oxygen" you need to breathe through the next eighteen to twenty-four months. Do not think you can cut all excess spending to get there more quickly; it is unrealistic and setting yourself up for failure.

For now, however, just focus on writing down everything you spend over the next month or two. Be gentle with yourself, and maybe two months in, you can tighten the belt a bit more. Then wait another couple of months, and see if you can tighten another notch. Budgets are not one and done, nor are they overnight success stories.

So, instead of giving you suggestions for things to think about trimming, I will remind you that you have already written down everything that you've spent and what you spent it on. You've taken ownership of this, and you are now informed as to how your spending has been channeled up to this point. When you review this to develop a budget, ask yourself:

- What do I want?
- What am I willing to give up to get what I want?

From there, review your spending habits and ask yourself:

- Where do I see excess?
- What spending is unnecessary?
- What is reasonable for me to let go of?
- What can be scaled down or cut back?
- What can be done less expensively?

If you need another way of doing this, just fill in the blank for each expenditure: *Do I really need to spend* _____ *on* _____? *Why or why not?*

Budgets are the beginning, the discovery of finding out where every cent is going. As you write down your transactions, you will see categories developing. You will start realizing things like, "Wait, I forgot about my nieces' and nephews' birthdays; I usually spend about a hundred bucks, so I need a category for birthdays, and determine if I need to adjust the dollar amount."

It is important to delegate every dollar to one of these categories. Within the categories, you will also see that some are needs, and some are wants; it is important that *needs* move up the priority list. Be honest with yourself on the differences between the two—you do not need to spend $200 on cosmetics if you are behind on your mortgage. Remember, you have to tell your money where to go; it cannot navigate itself!

If you have been writing everything down, you are picking up another skill: how to balance a checkbook and bank register. Many of us no longer use checks, so therefore, we do not know how to balance and reconcile it with our bank statements. We just debit, think we have a rough idea of what is in the bank, and are shocked when we are hit with a $40 insufficient funds charge. We forget about certain transactions, or our bank's online system does not operate in real time and we think something has cleared when it hasn't. This is another trap within financial bondage. Overdraft charges hurt, cost you more money, and exponentially increase your stress.

Stacy and Jason (not their real names) came to me for help. They were newlyweds who, prior to pooling their finances, had been used to debiting what they wanted out of their accounts. Many times, Jason found himself trusting the gas station attendant to let him know if his account was too low to cover his purchase, since most pumps pre-authorize purchases. Stacy usually gave a cursory glance at her checking account, making a mental note if things "looked" right.

They combined their accounts after they married, anticipating they would have a lot more money that way. But once their money had been combined, no one was writing in debits and keeping the checkbook balanced. Unfortunately, they were embarrassed when local vendors returned their bounced checks; they had also racked up considerable overdraft charges. In fact, Jason was refused a soda after he had poured it at a local gas station and attempted to pay with his debit card. Talk about "no soda for you"! It was terrible.

Stacy and Jason had not even been married a year. It was not long before they were fighting and felt inundated with problems. They did not have to face any of this before, when they were both single. Getting married includes many new adventures and added stressors, but insufficient funds should not be one of them.

Cash does hurt when you spend it, but you know exactly what you have. And cash is far less painful than the persistent stranglehold of financial bondage. Budgets work, as long as they are reasonable and kept up. I do not use a budget app personally, but my son Logan uses one, and it works well for him. If it keeps you on-budget, by all means, use an app. Bottom line: you just need to understand how much you have coming in, and how much you have going out. When you understand this, you will know the amount of money available to spend on non-necessities.

Apps, spreadsheets, even old-fashioned pencil and paper, the vehicle you use to get you there is not as important as committing to it. So if you are still unsure of how to organize your budget, use the sample I have provided in the "Additional Resources" section to get started. Feel free to tweak it to your personal situation; adapt it to your spreadsheet, app, spiral-bound notebook, chisel and stone tablets, whatever will help you achieve your goal of financial freedom instead of bondage.

If all of your bills are due at the same time, try to stagger them to correspond with paycheck deposits, getting the "biggies" out of the way first (like mortgage/rent). You may have to make a few phone calls to see what your options are, and you may be surprised at how many companies will work with you to stagger your bills with different due dates. Remember to list *all* the bills for this to be accurate. My husband was paid monthly and I was paid biweekly for many years. You may be paid differently. Take this into account when you are tweaking the example I have provided.

Sample Budget

MONTHLY BUDGET						
	Income - 1		1107.^{23}		1107.^{23}	
	Income - 2			3286.^{17}		
Expenses	**BUDGET**					
Mortgage / Rent			875.^{00}			
Church / Tithe			500.^{00}			
Car Payment		356.^{28}				
Insurance/House/Car			301.^{82}			
Life Insurance				64.^{00}		
Child Support						
Savings						
Allowance/Spend ✉		220.^{00}		220.^{00}		
Electric/Water/Trash			400.^{00}			
Gas/Fuel/House			57.^{00}			
Water / Garbage						
Telephone		180.^{00}				
Gas /Auto Expenses			400.^{00}			
Food ✉		100.^{00}	150.^{00}	200.^{00}		
Eat Out ✉		100.^{00}	150.^{00}	100.^{00}		
Snack & Lunch						
Personal						
Childcare						
Household ✉		100.^{00}	50.^{00}	100.^{00}		
Clothes			100.^{00}			
Medical/Dental			110.^{00}			
School / Lunch				50.^{00}		
Recreation / Cable				79.^{17}		
Haircuts ✉			90.^{00}			
Extra $ Towards Debt		50.^{95}	102.^{35}	214.^{06}		
Internet				80.^{00}		
Total =		1107.^{23}	3286.^{17}	1107.^{23}		
Envelope Money ✉		520.^{00}	440.^{00}	620.^{00}		

✉ = Those categories we used cash for

Don't Overcomplicate This!

Budgeting requires a cash flow plan every month, based on how often you are paid and how much money is coming in. I like cash, because it hurts more than a debit or credit card. Remember those stories of how my kids viewed the source of money? One saw me use cash, another saw me use checks, another saw me use an ATM, and finally, the fourth one saw me using a debit or credit card. The checking account must be balanced, and ATM, debit, and credit card purchases can quickly become budget-busters. If you want to get on track, this is going to require some concentrated effort by every individual who dips into your household fund. It is important not to leave things out. Please do not overcomplicate this, or you will never do it.

The bottom line is that managed money goes further. When you set aside money for variable expenses, like eating out, groceries, and household items, you will see how much further it goes once it is managed. Some people designate envelopes, some use accordion files—whatever system gets every cent assigned and accounted for gives you a leg up for staying on track.

You will soon learn what you are spending and more readily see problem areas and make some changes there. Let's say you are paid every fourteen days. You would want to develop a fourteen-day plan for your budget, telling every cent where to go. Now you will notice when you are running out of "eating-out money" by day eight of your fourteen-day plan. One of two things will occur: either you will realize that you are not putting enough money there, or you will realize that you are spending much more in that category than you thought. This is how we change direction. The decision is yours to make. You might have to change the amount going into the categories or move cash between funds and/or envelopes to make it last for two weeks or until your next paycheck.

There will be expenses that come up over the course of a few months, things you were not counting on that might change your budget.

Remember, we want to take quick, massive action. If you can plan your budget for thirty days and stick to it, you will start to see some success and want to keep doing it.

You will see on my budget example on the previous page where I had a category for extra expenditures, because we knew that some money needed to be held for things that we did not account for, things that we would normally put on our credit card. These categories could vary as you near the end of the pay period.

It's worth repeating: cash envelopes are a good choice for those expenditures that vary. We have four categories that we contributed cash to every two weeks, which is how often I got paid. These categories could vary quite significantly, and putting cash in an envelope helped us stay within the budget we wanted for these categories. They also gave us a visual.

Those categories were:

- Groceries
- Eating out
- Household goods
- Personal spending

This allowed us to see what we were spending and make choices. We might choose to move money from groceries to eating out or decide we could only order a pizza, not go to a sit-down restaurant, prior to the next payday. The money could be moved between envelopes or saved up for a fancy dinner if we wanted. This worked well for us! It made us stop and think if we really needed something or could make do until the next payday. For you, it might be the difference between eating frozen pizza versus eating in a restaurant, but it still gives you control over it.

Now, maintaining your budget is definitely going to get easier after your debt gets paid off, but it is crucial to tackle your spending. That doesn't mean quit your fun, cold turkey. You need to have some spending money; otherwise, it is unrealistic and just will not work. If your budget does not allow for any cash in your wallet to buy a Diet Coke or a trinket that you want, it just will not work. The trick is to try and lower these petty expenses, but they will not (and should not) disappear altogether. Again, keep it simple and do not overcomplicate it.

So what does that look like in real life? Maybe take leftovers most days for lunch, and go out to lunch on Fridays. Or maybe find cheaper places to eat out. You could clip coupons, shop and plan meals based on the sales ad at the supermarkets, and look for restaurant specials to help you stay on track, if overspending on food is an issue. It takes a little bit of planning, but it makes it so enjoyable when you get a good deal on something, and it keeps your budget on track.

If you think outside the box, and prioritize some categories, you can still enjoy life even in the process of releasing yourself from financial bondage. By telling your money where to go and giving every dollar a name, you will have a grasp on your spending. If you decide to keep spending $700 a month on restaurants and that leaves you nothing to contribute toward retirement, you can do that. But if that were me, I would be saying, "Okay, Brad, we are eating our retirement here."

At the very least, just know where your money is going. If you know that saving for retirement is a priority and you want to put fifty bucks toward it each month, then you look for the best places to pull from to get that fifty bucks together. This is so simple. So please, if you do nothing else, find out where your money is going. When you know, then you can make an informed decision. There are so many that do not know where their money goes, and they may blame it on each other, utilities, or everyday expenses, or they will just say they don't know. The interesting part of this is that your money may be going to places that you do not want it to go. With a few simple changes, you can direct it where you do want it to go.

If you are wondering about your spending decisions, and if money seems to burn a hole in your pocket, stay with me here, because the four steps comprise an actual money *plan*—a strategy to get you out of financial bondage. When you are headed in that direction, when you have a strategy, your job takes on a whole new meaning. At that point, you are *working* the plan, and it is a plan that works. It is so powerful.

If you start investing for retirement, your life is going to be so much better and more secure. You will be a better steward of what has been given to you and lose a lot of your taste for expensive things. And in time, you will have the peace that others do not understand. You will be able to help others with your abundance. This is what makes me tick.

Consider the Health Benefits

There is so much indebtedness in America right now that the things we own seem to own us. I can almost guarantee that you know someone (or maybe you yourself) who looks rich or has a great income, but they are stressed to the max in debt. When you are poor both on paper and in your heart, it can make you sick. You can't help others, although your heart wants to.

There are so many medical diseases that start with chronic stress, maybe all of them. This is the root cause of many medical diseases. I believe we could clear out many of the hospitals if we eliminated unresolved stress. As a medical professional, I have to touch on this aspect, because I have seen (and experienced) firsthand the detriment stress does to a body. Many times, I have seen patients who are the breadwinners in their family work nonstop to ensure they live well. They live in a big home and buy lots of nice gadgets. Quite often, the breadwinner may not even be able to enjoy what he or she has bought, because it's not paid for yet. There may be many loans and payments on the books. Then they have a heart attack or develop a health condition from all the stress and the increased cortisol levels. Their house of cards starts to tumble.

In data published by the Centers for Disease Control and Prevention, the American Heart Association says that 40–50 percent of patients will die with their very first heart attack. Too often, we are unhappy with our jobs because they are just covering all of our stressed-out bills. We feel like we are working for nothing, treading water just to keep the wolves on the bank of the river. Don't let this be you for a moment longer.

Think of it this way: if you get your debt under control, it will not only give you more peace, but potentially fewer medical bills and sick days. Start now—start writing down your spending to figure out how you will organize your budget. Yes, it can take a couple of months to tweak here and there, until you realize the categories you need to assign your spending. Sometimes what we think we're spending is not what we are spending at all. Then you will tweak those delegated amounts, because each category needs money going into it, and you do not know the exact amount each one needs to keep the household sustained. It might be different amounts, but you should have something in each one. This helps keep the budget realistic and workable.

Look, there are truly poor people in this country. Then there are those who are poor because they are driving expensive cars, living in fancy houses, and eating at pricey restaurants when they simply do not have the money to pay for all of it. They are putting their lives on plastic. When you think that a budget means that you will never be able to buy anything you want ever again, you are on the wrong path. It is the exact opposite. A budget will allow you to have what you want in an organized fashion that will not cause stress. When you tell your money where to go, magic can happen—including better physical, mental, and spiritual health. Do what others don't want to do now, so you can have what others won't have later.

What Living Within Your Means Really Means

Simply put, living within your means really means that you are living within your current salary. You have taken the guesswork out of borrowing from Peter to pay Paul for tomorrow. You are not living for a job that may never materialize, or a raise that may never arrive. Instead, you are writing down what you have coming in, and keeping up with every dime of it.

The Census Bureau data from 2020 shows the average household income in the United States is around $60,000, and there are people who have made this amount or less who have become millionaires. So if you live below your means and learn to say, "No, that's not in our budget, we're going to do it this way," you can still have a happy, peaceful, content life. Even if you make $30,000, you can still have a good life—if you spend based on that $30,000 budget. You can still give some to your church, have money put aside to help your children with college costs, or whatever categories your budget requires, but the lower your salary range, the more frugal and creative you will need to be to live the life of your dreams!

We have lost the art of frugality, because we think it is too painful and we "want ours now," so to speak. There is always a way to find a better way, a better deal, a better price.

For example, we want to skip the starter home and go straight to the McMansion, because that is what Mom and Dad have. Likely, Mom and Dad also qualified for a better interest rate, no PMI (private mortgage insurance), and worked their way up to a nicer house. So now, you have these massive mortgage payments that don't fit in your budget or salary at all, because you trusted the guy at the bank who told you what you could afford. Trust me, that guy did not factor in your retirement contributions or your child's tuition when he came up with that number.

When you live within your means, you live with and live on the amount of money you have coming in at that given time. It should cover the bills and allow you some fun, too. When you are in the process of righting the ship to live within your means, you feel like your money is being put to good use; you may barely make it work, but you are making it work. And when it works, it changes your whole mindset, your entire outlook on life.

If you have a plan for what you are going to do with your money, it puts you in the top 10 percent of U.S. families, and this can change your life in eighteen to twenty-four months. So, if you know how much you need in each category, now is the time to put it on paper. Some of your expenses are set amounts, and others will be educated guesses that get better over time.

How to Balance a Checkbook

I do not care if you use a debit card or cash app exclusively, your bank still provides you a check register, and balancing your checkbook is still relevant. Why? Because you also have to reconcile it with your bank statement.

I am old-fashioned in the sense that I still break out the paper register and reconcile with a paper statement that is mailed to me. You may prefer to do these things online, but they still need to be done. You need to be able to get into your checking and savings accounts to see what is going on with them. This is part of being a good steward of your finances. Although rare, banks can make costly mistakes if they are not caught. Your account could get hacked. Keeping an eye on things can alert you earlier when a problem exists.

Make sure that everything is on the up and up with your bank statement, but you also need to make sure that every debit is yours, regardless of whether the transaction was paid via app, plastic, or cash. If you bought clothes at a store and paid with cash, document this in the register to help you sustain your budget. Look at the variable bills that occur each month, like utilities; figure out how to average that bill so that you have budgeted a reasonable amount to cover it when it is higher, and replenish it when it is lower. Some utility companies have programs that let you pay an average amount year-round, and settle up during the twelfth month (they may owe you, or you may owe them, so watch your usage to be ready!).

I have provided a sample checkbook register here that shows you how to add and subtract to balance and reconcile your checking account. Doing this will help you see what is really happening.

# OR CODE	DATE	TRANSACTION DESCRIPTION	PAYMENT AMOUNT	✔	FEE	DEPOSIT AMOUNT	BALANCE	
CK#	5/1/21	**STARTING BALANCE**					*286*	*33*
314	5/1/21	XYZ ELECTRIC COMPANY	128 OO				-128	OO
							158	*33*
DD	5/1/21	ABC EMPLOYER				1107 23	+1107	23
CK#							*1265*	*56*
315	5/4/21	PEKIN LIFE INSURANCE	64 OO				-64	OO
							1201	*56*
AD	5/5/21	NETFLIX	18 OO				-18	OO
							1183	*56*
DC	5/6/21	GROCERY STORE	85 93				-85	93
							1097	*63*

DD = DIRECT DEPOSIT, AD = AUTOMATIC DEBIT, DC = DEBIT CARD

If you learn how to do this, and stay disciplined enough to actually do it, you will stop glancing and thinking, *that looks about right*, to actually knowing whether it *is* correct. If this is your first real attempt at balancing a checkbook, I do recommend starting with a paper checkbook register so you can see it on paper in the beginning. You can get these free from the bank. You will need to check these online every three to five days, but eventually you should be able to do this every two weeks or even monthly.

Honestly, this is another reason why it is a good idea to go to a cash-envelope system for some categories of expenses, particularly those small impulse buys. Really, who wants to document every pack of gum you buy on the fly at the convenience store when you can designate a cash envelope for these sorts of things? That way, you have already debited the *total amount budgeted* from your account; the twenty or so impulse buys like that pack of gum are pulled from the cash envelope instead of your debit card. That is much simpler, isn't it? If you are an overachiever, you can always hang on to the receipts to review your cash spending and tweak your budget for the next pay period.

Cash and receipts are much simpler than a ton of debits in the long run. They provide an extra checkpoint for your spending. They eliminate the embarrassment of a cashier telling you that your card was declined. If your budget allows $100 for groceries, and you have that in cash tucked away in an envelope, you can do the mental tally to spare you that experience. Once you have checked out, tuck the receipt into your cash envelope to see if you can trim it next time, make sure the store did not make any errors, and keep a record of the incidentals you paid for with your cash.

It's important that someone is balancing the checkbook, even online. You will avoid overdraft charges and embarrassment. When you put cash in envelopes for certain expenses, it will mean less worry about balancing those numbers in the checkbook.

How Often Will Your Budget Change?

"Why can't I just make one budget and be done with it?"

This is a question I am often asked, and to tell you the truth, I wish it worked like that. Life does not work like that, so neither will your budget. Remember that eventually some of this will become almost a reflex, and you will not have to think as hard about every action or transaction. But just like learning anything new, you will need to make a conscious effort at first—quick, massive action is the key. Like taking medicine, get it over with and do this important step! I would recommend re-examining your budget on a weekly basis until you have a true grasp of spending. Get into the habit of documenting and having a better handle on what should be paid with cash. You don't know what you don't know, and until you are actively doing these things, you will not find out.

Most of the time things creep up on us, things we did not even account for. If you pay your insurance every six months or annually, for example, you might forget to budget a portion of it monthly. You also need time to learn which categories have too much or too little in your budget, and figure out where money may be "hidden" to pay off debt. (We will get more into that in the next chapter. Trust me, it will be fun!)

Eventually, you will get to a point where your budget is more on-point and calms down so you can shift to changing it on a monthly basis, then a quarterly basis, and maybe even a biannual/annual basis. This takes time and practice. And there is no shame in deciding that you just need to stick with reviewing it on a monthly basis.

Let's be clear, however, about the temptation to change your budget when it *should not* be changed. Let's say you find a $4,000 sofa on sale for $1,500. You love the sofa, and it's such a good deal. You think, *Maybe my budget's gonna change right there on the spot.* Nope. I don't recommend that at all, not on an impulse buy like that. I would even say use online "wish lists" when you want to make purchases that aren't necessities, or keep them in your cart for twenty-four to forty-eight hours. See if you still want that item as much as you did two days ago...or can you wait a bit longer before you purchase?

Your budget should be fluid, so that as you pay down your debt, you can change it. The amount you add to categories can then increase, or you can add new categories or pay off more debt. Remember, you decide where your money goes, and wouldn't it be great to free up some cash to get into the next step?

You're still wondering when you can get the sofa, aren't you?

Unless it is a necessity (house, utilities, car, or food), hold off at least in the first eighteen months while you are getting debt paid off. After that, you can decide where extra money goes. There will always be another sofa on sale.

This may seem like an obvious question, but how will you know if your budget is working? If you have enough to cover your expenses and you can see some money freeing up that we will soon apply to debt, without incurring more debt right now, then your budget is working. The byproducts of a working budget are peace and confidence, and you will see light at the end of the tunnel. It is not going to happen right away; there may be months where there is not enough to cover certain things, or you have to dip into your emergency fund. You may have minor setbacks, but remember that you took a giant step forward. Commit to replenish that emergency money, and get right back on track.

Keep on Giving, Regardless

For most of us, generosity produces good feelings. We like to be known as generous, and sometimes we get hooked on the good feelings and give more than we really have.

Giving is a very personal decision, but I would never encourage a giver to refrain while they are getting their finances in order. We are all here on this earth for a reason, and there is always someone in our sphere who could use a helping hand. There is always someone worse off than you, whether it is physical, spiritual, emotional, or financial health. If you can't give money, can you give time to help? Can you babysit for somebody for free? Can you help somebody clean something up and not accept payment? Do you have an extra set of bunk beds that you can give to a family in need of beds? Can you lend an ear to a friend who is grieving? We all have a need to give to others. I believe you always get more than you give. Keep an open hand on giving and receiving—so it can flow freely, back and forth. That is the magic of the universe.

No matter what you have, you should be generous. This does not mean that you give away the hundred dollars that was meant for your electric bill, or you give away the only extra twenty dollars you have that month. There is something about an open heart that is willing to give, so budget for this amount, however small—you are going to give plenty when you have more to give.

Remember Brady and Sandra? I told you they worked it out, but what exactly was their happy ending? They ended up staying together and moving to Florida, where they said they always wanted to live. It was a dream of theirs. They both found jobs and love it down there. They are still married, and still very much in love. Their daughter is married now too, and Brady and Sandra are grandparents. They own two cars and a house and take a yearly vacation. They are not wealthy by worldly means, but their lives have been transformed by no longer living in financial bondage. That is true wealth!

You do not have to live in bondage, either. Are you ready to be released? Every dollar goes somewhere, whether you name it or not. You can research and study all the different financial plans or what people did, while the debt and the confusion pile up instead of the money. I have done the work for you, and the four-step plan works. Now it is time to give every dollar a name, so get ready, because some of them will be named *debt*.

WANNA HAVE FUND$?

Figure out a way to give back that doesn't cost you money, but fills up your heart. Can you do this regularly?

CHAPTER 5

Step Three: Climb Aboard the Debt Locomotive

I LOVE THE PICTURE BOOK *THE LITTLE ENGINE THAT COULD*. WHEN MY children were little, it was a favorite bedtime story, so I read it to them all the time. The little engine did not think she could make it up a steep hill to deliver food and toys to all the good little children on the other side of the mountain. If you read the story, everything is good and bright. The toys are friendly, and those little kids are depending on them. When the little engine's thoughts told her she couldn't make it up the hill, she didn't. But when she told herself, "I think I can, I think I can," she could, and did. As my children grew up and they faced discouragement—maybe in sports or dealing with social issues—I would say, "Remember the little engine that could," and they would look at me with determination and try again. Sometimes, they would actually say out loud, "I think I can."

I revisited the story while writing this book, and though I'd read it for many years to my children, only now did I realize that the story actually refers to the little blue engine as "she"—I mean, that was like a flipping lightbulb moment for me. It turned out to be a female engine that was willing to give it a try. She pulled and pulled, encouraging herself with her voice chugging, "I think I can, I think I can," over and over. And you know the rest of the story. (Spoiler alert: *she did.*)

I use this story to coach others, particularly women, to tackle their debt and set themselves financially free. When I discovered that the little engine that could (and *did*) was actually female, it reinforced my resolve to persist in teaching women to take control of their finances.

Do You Think *You* Can?

When it comes to tackling debt or any other big challenge, if your thoughts say you can't, you won't. So regardless of what your current situation is, you have to change your thinking. When we look at people who failed many times, but then succeeded with a career goal, it was because of their thinking and persistence. Many of them will say they knew something good was going to happen, they just had to keep working at it. Eliminating your debt is no different. You have to not only *think* it, but *believe* it. You can and will reduce your debt, little by little, chugging right along. There is so much power in positive thinking; people are capable of more than they ever imagine! You have to believe it, then put the effort in to achieve it.

There are two sides to this, because there is also power in negative thinking—but it is negative power, not positive power. *I can never do this* speaks for itself. It stops you in your tracks. Why would you put effort, time, and energy into something you feel you won't succeed at? Also, words have power. Refrain from using or listening to negative words.

We need to explore the mind and the power that it holds. We need to set aside what others might have told us that we absorbed and believed about ourselves. In fact, we also have to overcome our own negative self-talk that sabotages what we really want.

All it takes is one small thing to go wrong, the straw to break the camel's back, and the stress of all that debt becomes your constant companion. When it happens, you can't concentrate on the good things around you. Your job becomes a burden because you think you are not paid enough to cover all of these bills, and you are right. Or worse, you work only to pay bills, with nothing left over for fun or your future.

As debt becomes the source of our stress, all expenses, even expected things like new school clothes, dig the hole deeper. Most of us in medicine know that stress increases our cortisol levels, which decreases our immunity. This can make us physically sick. When we don't feel well, even mentally (because of the financial stress), we tend to take this out on those we love the most. We are less loving toward other adults in our household, because we hold a grudge or resent their lack of contribution, thinking either they do not make enough money or should spend less. There is stress associated with the costs of caring for loved ones and pets. We forgo our own doctor and dental appointments, which makes our own health suffer. This is a perfect storm for feeling helpless and hopeless.

Even if you have a trusted friend or relative who does not think you can do this, you still get to decide for yourself. You do not have to be rude to them, just chug away at what I am about to tell you and keep going. True wealth is within your grasp, and while that may not always mean "rolling in money," you can work to be very comfortable and enjoy this life. Start by believing that there are great and mighty plans for you. You can start anytime, but why not start now?

You have already succeeded in socking away about $2,000 into your emergency fund, right? That is Step One in the plan.

You are living within your means based on the budget you developed, right? That is Step Two in the plan.

Now, you start Step Three, climbing aboard the debt locomotive, getting rid of debt. *You can do this!*

The Little Engine That Could gained steam as she moved up that hill. When she reaches its pinnacle, she glides over the top and it is smooth sailing the rest of the way. When you get moving on your debt and pay some of it off, your momentum increases. Just like a powerful locomotive, this will propel you forward even faster. You will be able to do great things when you're not strapped down with debt. It is such a heavy burden on the mind and the body, like an invisible noose around your neck. Even my oldest granddaughter, Brooklyn, understands how great it feels to be unburdened; when she was younger, she would run up and down our hallway after her bath yelling, "I'm debt free!" It is never too early to plant precious seeds like this in a child's mind.

Maybe your debt started at a young age, with student loans. Or maybe you have been strapped with debt most of your adult life, you have accepted it will always be with you. Look, the little engine had never been over the mountain. All that she knew was on her side of the mountain, but she thought she could do it. She decided it might not be that unreasonable for her to attempt it. She thought she could. So she did.

Is Debt Ever Necessary or Positive?

Is there ever a case where debt should be necessary, ordinary, or even positive? The short answer to that is *yes*. Debt can be positive when it is in some form of a car payment or a mortgage (I don't necessarily consider rent as a form of debt). What we have actually all been taught, however, is that the American Dream consists of one house, two cars, a yearly vacation, and the lifetime of payments that go along with these! There is certainly nothing wrong with wanting those things, or attaining them. It might come, but it comes with a hefty price tag, one that usually requires financing.

Few of us can write a legit check to pay for a vehicle in full, much less a home. Remember the four necessities we talked about earlier? Two of these were a home and reliable transportation, and sometimes, that means a small car payment and a mortgage. Some debt may be necessary, for now, but it does not have to mean that you enter into retirement with a mortgage and two car payments.

Here are a few more facts:

- If you want to spend everything you make now, then you will have to work harder, longer.

- If you can save some now for the future, you can retire earlier or move into a part-time or dream career.

- If you reduce, and even eliminate, your debt now, you open up a world of options and opportunities with regard to how long and how hard you *choose* to work.

There is a big difference, and a major shift in perspective, when work is a matter of choice instead of a necessity. Moving the needle on debt puts you back in the driver's seat.

So in terms of getting out of it, how do we get out of it? Hammer away at it all at once? Prioritize it? Is there a pecking order that we should apply when we are talking about getting out of debt?

Start Small, Gain Momentum

Before we start tackling your debt, we have to know what we are dealing with here. This is not easy, because it requires you to face some painful reality. This is where I want you to go old-school, with pen and paper, to create your Debt Locomotive Model. (See following page.)

List all of your revolving debt (not mortgage) on one sheet of paper. In the left column, list all the retailers, credit cards, furniture and electronics, and vehicles you owe on. Make sure you list them all, even any money borrowed from family. Do not include your variable expenses, like utilities. These expenses are ongoing and should be part of your monthly budget. If you are not sure you have listed them all, run a free credit report on the adults in your household at annualcreditreport.com to ensure you have included them all. Make sure this credit report is accurate, and correct anything that is wrong.

In fact, quick detour: there are three different services where you can get a free credit report once a year. You could actually pick one service every four months to space out three copies over the course of a year. This will alert you to problems earlier. You may be reminded of a medical bill you did not know about, or maybe even discover an error on your credit record that affects your credit score.

Next, make two more columns that list the monthly minimum payments and outstanding balance for each debt. Take a hard look at this sheet; absorb its reality without judgment or shame. Release the part about *how* you got there, and commit your energy to getting out of it. Acknowledge that it is go-time.

I have already mentioned that there are a number of plans out there to manage your finances, and reducing/eliminating your debt is a key step in just about all of them. There are as many approaches to this step as there are plans. In Step Three of my plan, reducing your debt begins with paying off smaller debts first. There is a psychological reason for starting small; you will see some progress in a fairly short period of time, and that is very motivating. It will make you feel like you have accomplished something and motivate you to keep going.

Example of Debt Locomotive

DEBT LOCOMOTIVE

Item	Total Payoff	Minimum Payment	New Payment
Kohl's	297.^{76}	27.^{00}	
Target	380.^{59}	27.^{00}	
ABC Furniture	1237.^{22}	72.^{00}	
Barclay Visa	4509.^{60}	87.^{00}	
Citi card	5896.^{28}	79.^{00}	
GMC Auto	8672.^{43}	356.^{28}	

For a blank copy, see the Additional Resources section.

Look at your Debt Locomotive Model sheet, and pick out the one debt with the smallest outstanding balance. Put down the monthly minimum on all the rest, then start tackling the smallest one first, paying more on this debt as you free up money. Do not get caught up in the interest rates of each bill, just take the smallest balance and work toward paying it off before all the others. Just like the little engine, you will gain momentum and move faster to climb up and over the hill one mile at a time. And what happens once the smallest debt is paid off?

You revisit your Debt Locomotive list, taking the money that was going toward that debt and directing those dollars to the next smallest debt, and so on. Maybe a few of those dollars land in your "blow money" envelope, if it was empty before this time. Why do I encourage this? Because I want you to have fun, stay engaged, and keep working on it. Now it may not be the same fun you were having, but with each bill that is paid off, the debt noose loosens a bit, allowing you to breathe and enjoy your current life right now.

You will make memories by thinking outside the box, forming different ideas of fun. Even mundane tasks or outings are more fun when they are not adding to your debt. I promise that being able to breathe, relax, and enjoy *is* fun.

You can still enjoy fine food, experiences, and getting away. Maybe instead of eating at an expensive restaurant, you can order take out and eat it near a lake or in the park. You can purchase a nice bottle of wine and treats from a gourmet shop for a picnic. If you are wanting to get away for a while, look at more localized adventures—camping, horseback riding in a park, an amusement park, fishing, hiking. Be careful here, because you can step back into overspending on these types of excursions, too. The idea is that you don't move backward, but still find ways to have some fun. Enlist friends to help. Do they have a lake house, pontoon, or fishing pond that your family could enjoy? I am writing this book right now while looking at the lake from my friends Linda and Scott's boathouse. It is free and very relaxing.

Does your neighborhood have a listserv or online forum? You could borrow or rent things instead of buying them, especially items that you may only use once or twice a year. You also save yourself any maintenance or upkeep, particularly if you opt to rent something like a pontoon boat or jet skis instead of buying them. We do this with our whole family once a year at a local lake.

There are other times when the extra dollars may not be about fun. Has your car spent too much time in the shop lately? Maybe it needs some money put toward big expenses so that they do not cost you more in the long run. If you need a different, more reliable car, buy a good used car that will last you a few years instead of having a big car payment on a newer model. It is not your forever vehicle, but it will get you through until your finances are in better shape.

I did not drive a minivan with a broken door for seventeen years without acknowledging that car payments can rob you of your retirement. At the same time, I'm not going to be unrealistic and say you cannot have a car payment. What I will say is that if you could only have one car payment per household at a time, your future life will be better. This also needs to be a reasonable amount, not $900 a month. If you must finance a vehicle, keep it at $400 or less a month. You can lower a car payment by initially putting more money down on the car. I will show you why I feel the way I do about car payments later.

Let's get back to the debt locomotive. You will start with paying off the smallest debt, working your way to paying off the largest debt. You will do this with any extra money that is left from your budget each pay period. With the exception of the one debt you are focused on paying off, make the minimum payments on each of the other debts. Now, for you overachievers out there, you may have the urge to stick another fifty bucks toward your Visa payment, even though the minimum is only $150. Instead, stick the extra fifty bucks on the debt you are paying off and just pay the minimum on the Visa until it is the smallest debt you have. Then, the extra money goes toward paying the Visa off. As you get it paid off, roll that payment into the next debt to tackle. As each debt is erased, you will literally feel the burden lifting from your shoulders, back, and gut.

Finally, the mortgage is usually your biggest expenditure, and many are okay with always having a mortgage payment, while others choose to pay it off after eliminating all other debt. We decided that was more important for us to do before we funded our children's college funds. This is a personal decision for you to make.

When you free up cash, you are going to start applying it to your debt. I like applying extra money to the smaller debts, regardless of the interest rates. This is where the debt locomotive becomes active and starts climbing the hill that you had previously thought was insurmountable. You keep applying more and more pressure to the debt and make some real progress. In time, that locomotive reaches the pinnacle of the hill, then glides over, heading you to financial freedom.

Other Ways to Reduce Debt

In addition to making actual payments, are there other ways to reduce debt? Yes, there are several.

Let's start with any vehicle you are currently making payments on. If your current car payment is above $400, find out if there is a way to refinance it to get that payment below $400. Or, like I mentioned earlier in the chapter, see if you can sell it and purchase a less expensive vehicle outright with the money from that sale. If that does not work for you, just place this vehicle payment in the debt locomotive and eliminate it when it becomes the smallest debt.

Why does it seem like I am always on the attack when it comes to vehicle payments? If there is any way that a family can stay away from two car payments or, even better, have no car payments at all, you will retire with money. I say it all the time: I believe that car payments rob us of our retirement. They only smell nice for a short period of time, especially if you have children. The average car depreciates 30-40 percent the first year you drive it off the lot, according to *Canadian Black Book*. Why not buy a nice used car and let someone else take that loss?

When it comes to finding other ways to reduce your debt, think outside the box here. Pull from some of my favorite strategies when you are paying down debt:

- Try "coupon eating," where you only eat at places when you have a coupon to apply toward the meal.

- Shop for items that you will always need—think paper products or cleaners—when you find them on sale.

- Drink water. At home, at work, and when you are out for a meal.

- Lower or stop internet service, cell phone, satellite TV, or other services and features that you do not really use, or could temporarily do without.

- Conserve on heating and air conditioning bills by setting your thermostat at the same temperature each season. Bundle up in the winter and strip off layers in the summer. We have an attic fan that cools things off cheaply in the spring and fall without turning on the air conditioner.

- Call creditors to see if you can lower the interest rate or payments. You would be surprised at how many are willing to work with you.

- Set up a "wishlist wait." We spend so much time on social media, looking at others' posts, and then we want an item they have or that we see advertised. We point, click, purchase without blinking an eye. Online retailers have rewritten the definition of *impulse buy* in that respect. Instead, set up a wishlist on the retailer's site and, when you point and click, save it to the wishlist. Give yourself at least forty-eight hours, if not longer, to make your purchasing decision. You may discover that the item you so desperately wanted two days ago no longer matters much to you.

We do not need all this stuff, and we certainly do not need it immediately. When we get our money in alignment with our spirit, we increase paying off the debt and learn how to save up to buy things. There is something so special about paying cash for a purchase or vacation. It makes it that much sweeter when it doesn't follow you around for two years or longer.

If we also take time to clean and organize our homes and care for our cars, I do not think we will want new ones as quickly, or think what we have are pieces of junk. We have to be good stewards of what we own, and take care of it, even down to the shoes on our feet. (By staying organized, you are also less likely to buy duplicates!)

As your debt locomotive gains momentum, your eyes will be peeled for ways to free up more cash, whether that means cutting out some things or selling others. You may keep taking your lunch to work or cut the cord on cable. Remember, this can be temporary or, if you find you do not miss it, just stay the course. If you are a good steward of what you have been given, success will follow. However you choose to do this, you are on your way to financial freedom.

What About Debt Reduction and Cash Advance Services?

It seems that everywhere you look on television, billboards, and online, there are services promising to consolidate, reduce, or completely wipe out your debt. Cash-advance services promise to get you through the month. Maybe you have made your list of debts and realized that they exceed what you are bringing in each month, and the temptation is to reach out to these types of services.

If this describes your situation, keep reading.

There is the phrase "desperate times call for desperate measures," and I would agree, but I caution you to choose your measures carefully. As much of an advocate as I am for contributing toward your retirement, this may be a good time to stop your contributions until you can pay down your debt. This is just temporary, very temporary.

Cash-advance services make it look and sound so easy and painless. The truth is, they charge high interest rates, huge late fees, and penalties. Talk about borrowing on your future! The high interest and fees will cost you dearly, more often than not. It is a terrible idea. A cash-advance fee might be 3 to 5 percent higher than the interest rate on your credit card. A few hundred dollars could feasibly take years to pay off, and they are set up to work that way.

If you are getting cash advances for regular purchases, there is no grace period. The interest accrues from the day you received the advance. So you think, I'll pay it in twenty days when my credit card bill comes due. Nope. You will see that charge plus interest on that charge from the day it was made. This never makes sense!

I feel the same way about debt-reduction and debt-consolidation services. Many of them cost money and possibly have some hidden fees to do things that you can actually do yourself, like call creditors and ask them to freeze your account, stop accruing interest, or take partial payments as payment-in-full. Before you think, "Wow, that sounds great! I would only pay a portion, and they forgive the rest," let me caution you that this type of arrangement does hit your credit score. Some will tell you that is no big deal because you are going to pay cash for everything moving forward, but I care about your credit score and recommend that you do, too. So if you can pay everything you owe in full, please do it. You are the one who racked up this debt.

When it comes to reducing large amounts of debt, there are no quick fixes. It is the tortoise and the hare—slow and steady will win the race. At the same time, I think quick, massive action is a great motivator. My method attacks the smallest balances first, regardless of the interest rate, to achieve the quickest results and keep you chugging along on the pathway to success. Many of these debt-reduction services promise to clean up your debt mess by working with your creditors, for a fee, and they are more than you would pay if you just kept chipping away at it yourself. I get it, it is scary to think about calling your creditors and, in a sense, asking a favor from them—but think of it this way: The worst they can say is *no*. Beyond that, they can't hurt you or affect your value as a human being. You will be surprised how accommodating they just might be. Most people avoid contacting them when they need help, just remain calm and reasonable during the conversation.

Debt consolidation combines all of your debt into a single debt as a settlement, usually at a lower interest rate. There are companies you can hire to provide this service and once it is done, it's considered a "debt settlement" that also affects your credit score. If you are truly desperate and cannot face your creditors, you can go this route, but in full disclosure, you can actually do this yourself. Some people transfer everything to a zero-percent promotional interest rate credit card, a home-equity line of credit, or some other type of loan. I want to throw out a couple of cautions before you travel down this road:

- If you have not cured or figured out what got you into this mess in the first place, you're going to get back in the same boat and;

- it will be worse, because if you haven't paid off your debt within a specified promotion period, you will pay interest on the full amount that you transferred, and;

- you'll be in debt even longer. How so?

Let's say you owe $30,000 in debt, which includes a two-year loan for $10,000 at a 12 percent interest rate and the payments are $471. You also have a four-year loan for $20,000 at 10 percent interest, that has a payment of $507. So you're paying $978 a month to cover those. After speaking with a debt-consolidation company, they can decrease your payment to $541 a month at a 9 percent interest rate, through negotiation. By rolling two loans into one, your payment is now $437 lower per month. That sounds great, doesn't it?

Here's the downside: You have six years to pay off the loan at this lower payment. And it costs you $3,000 more to pay these off over the life of the loan. That's a rip-off.

In Over Your Head? A Better Route

Look, one of the biggest favors you can do for yourself is to actually *get* outside help when you recognize that you need it. There are free consumer debt counselors in most areas, and they will spend time understanding your specific circumstances and help you organize a strategy, just like I am doing with you in this book. They will help you write out your debt, your budget, and your income, just like we are doing here, and encourage you when you have a manageable plan in place.

You can also do this yourself without being tricked into spending more money that you do not have. It will build your own confidence. When you DIY (do it yourself), you are less likely to repeat your spending offenses. I am outlining the proven steps in this book, showing you how to build a strategy.

Another favor you can do for yourself: Credit cards require responsibility, so you must stay organized and exercise some self-control and self-discipline in order to maintain responsible parameters—your credit score, stress levels, and ability to do other things with your money hang in the balance. Frankly, I love having a credit card, but I pay it off each month. That is why I will not tell you to cut them up or freeze them in a block of ice. If you discover you are one of those who cannot manage your spending, however, you may need to get rid of your credit cards altogether.

Borrowing from Peter to pay Paul is a risky, stressful game, and yes, we all know many people who are doing it. No matter our income, we can live within or below our means and attain the peace that everybody longs for. It is the peace that no expensive meal, no article of clothing, and no new car can satisfy.

Get Out, and Stay Out!

So now that you are out of debt, how do you stay out? You rename the "freedom money" you are saving, over and over again. This may even require a few new categories in your budget—down payments for cars, new furniture, Christmas gifts, birthday parties, power tools, camping gear, infrequent expenses like car insurance, license plates, property taxes, school clothes—so that none of these catch you by surprise. Commit to put none of these expenses on a credit card so you can stick with your budget. When the debt locomotive has gotten over the hill, you will start putting money into these funds.

I happen to have a credit union that automatically distributes money from my paycheck into designated savings funds, like property taxes, license plates, vacation, Christmas, all of it. This is done automatically, and I do not even have to think about it.

The biggest thing to remember is that now that you have made it here, do not slide back into debt. Save up for things. Do not acquire more payments! This has been hard work, no sense in doubling your efforts. You do not want to work your way out of there again. What do you do when you have all your debts paid off, minus maybe a small car payment and your mortgage? That is the million-dollar question. You have a decision here. My advice is to build up that emergency fund to include three to six months of living expenses. If you have been working a part-time job to drive your debt locomotive, maybe keep working there to build up your savings. This savings will bring you peace from fear of the unknown—like a sickness, job loss or change, or any major unexpected expense.

When the debt locomotive has cleared the hill, women feel more secure. It is just who we are. Knowing that even if something unexpected happens, we can still pay the bills for a few months, is just so reassuring. Our mindset regarding our job changes. We do not cling so tightly to it that we're impossible to work with, and we are better at what we do because we know that we do not "have" to work there if we want to take time off or search for another job entirely. I believe you can start enjoying what you do for a living even more when you realize that you are saving for your future dreams. Your job is funding the life you desire right now. Enjoy every minute of it.

When you work these steps, you will move much more quickly to get there, and once you have arrived, you'll discover something else: the thrill is not found in how much your bank account has accrued, but rather in how hard you worked to get there. Enjoy the process, and enjoy the journey. You are learning a lot about money...and about yourself.

I have witnessed those who have worked the four steps, gotten control of their finances, and subsequently were blessed beyond measure. You will see this magic happen in your own journey. Many times, your debt will be paid off more quickly than you could imagine. By being a good steward, your cup of joy overflows. When you are doing the best you can with what money has been entrusted to you, really putting some effort into it, your financial freedom often happens sooner than you think. Regardless, this is a small amount of time in comparison to the rest of your life.

Be aware that your budget may fail you many times. History is full of success stories that really boil down to the person's persistence through many failures. Knowing what you want, and focusing on that one thing (getting out of debt), is the most important step in developing this type of persistence. A strong desire can help you overcome many obstacles. Napoleon Hill, author of *Think and Grow Rich*, once said that most ideas just need the breath of life injected into them through definite plans of immediate action.

Life coach Tony Robbins also says the same thing this way: "When you find what it is you want, take quick, massive action toward accomplishing it." When you do this, you accelerate your dreams and them happening much more quickly.

If you know that you are doing your best, this also means that sometimes you should just slow down and rest. Speeding through this whole process will bring only sorrow. Slow down today to be happy tomorrow. If we sacrifice a little now, we can live differently later. We will not have to work forever, or try to get help from the government or our children when we retire. Enjoy this process.

Let me repeat, you will not live like this forever, unless you choose to. When you get out of this, you will be able to have things you want instead of them having you. When the debt locomotive gathers steam, you will still enjoy what you are doing *now* even more, and can plan on an even brighter future. All aboard!

WANNA HAVE FUND$?

Congratulations! You're out of debt. In the 2018 National Financial Capability Study conducted by the FINRA Foundation, 46 percent of Americans don't have a rainy day fund that would cover three months of expenses. Now it's time to go back and revisit your emergency fund—set a goal to save enough money to cover three months' worth of expenses. Set mini-goals of $500 increments until you get there (and don't stop when you do!)

CHAPTER 6

Step Four: Retirement

A LOT OF COUPLES COME TO ME FOR FINANCIAL COUNSELING. SOME ARE older than me and are nearing retirement. They are doing well in society's eyes, but have never been taught these four steps. Bart and Lori (not their real names) were this couple. They were wanting to retire in a year or so, but when they looked at their retirement income, they realized they would bring in less during retirement than they were currently bringing in actively working. They had saved hard for retirement and made big plans for travel and leisure. They had talked in-depth about what their plans were, because they were actually going to be retiring a little earlier than most other people. If they stayed the course, they would have to take quite a bit of money from their other saved funds each month to cover the retirement they were dreaming of. Bart realized they needed to change course, and do so quickly.

"We have been planning this all along. How can we change it within a year of retirement?" Lori asked with concern. Initially, Bart was upset, too, because he had wanted to see his grandkids more and play more golf. Their two grown daughters were also upset, because they needed grandparents to help with babysitting.

Bart and Lori had a lot of big questions to ask themselves and needed to make some tough decisions, but their story is not all that unusual. We tend to think that we have planned for our retirement, do our best to be careful with our money, think we are doing okay, and then we run numbers close to retirement that might lead us to a different conclusion. Their big issue was that they still had two car payments and a mortgage payment. Bart had been taught that you always have those payments.

As we run the numbers to get a realistic perspective on our retirement, many of us wonder how we will make it on less income as we inch closer to what should be a great season of life. We have not thought too much about it until we are in the final stretch, continuing to live on whatever we bring home, no matter which kids are still living at home or what has already been paid off. We do not really, truly "plan" for retirement, we just have this idea that one day, we will flip the switch from working to no longer working, and everything else will remain the same, in terms of income. We always think retirement is so far away, until it is not. Most of us have not considered that this sort of plan may include a significant pay cut.

This is why it is always best to earmark your money and have it do what you really want it to do—including those dollars that should go toward your retirement. By implementing the four-step plan I am outlining, you can be financially ahead of 90 percent of the people working their way through life. You have a plan, and you are working on it. You want to do better than previous generations of your family and live the *true* American Dream, not the facade that is propped up by debt and frivolous spending.

Life is meant to be lived, and you are well on your way to living it! The four steps take this into account; there are some sacrifices, but there are still opportunities for fun and leisure.

Is It Ever Too Late to Start?

I am often asked if it is too late to start saving for retirement, and my answer is always the same: *never*.

Of course, the earlier you start, the better off you will be. Whether you start in your twenties, thirties, forties, or fifties, the important thing is to start *now*. I do not care if you are going to retire in a year and you are saving fifty bucks a month. Do it. It is that much more money you will have waiting for you.

Another question I'm asked: *how do I know if I am saving enough for retirement?* And that is the question of all questions. The truth is, no one really knows the exact figures each one of us needs. Many people are advised that if they have a million dollars saved, they are going to be fine. As someone who has been unable to buy a pizza, I can honestly say that saving a million dollars is just not realistic for many of us. And who knows how far a million will go in a future economy? If you are in your early fifties, a million dollars is a really high number to save, even if you work another twenty years.

The trick is to push your way into saving more and more. As you get your finances in order, you will feel less stress when you think about retirement. Why? Your household can handle emergencies, has an "operating budget," and you are chipping away at debt. Each month, each year, you have a clearer picture and can better assess if you can live on what is coming in. You can project, or estimate, what you will have coming in during retirement from Social Security, possibly a pension, and withdrawals from whatever money you have saved. The universal recommendation during retirement is not to draw more than 4 percent per year of what you have saved to live on, if you want it to last.

Beyond that, there is no universal estimate for the exact amount each person needs, money-wise. Will you live in the Midwest, or in a big coastal city? Does your state tax retirement income? Is your house paid off? Do you want to travel? If so, do you want to travel by car, by plane, or maybe by RV? Will you travel overseas, or just around the United States? Many factors can be changed to make sure your retirement is all you want it to be, and those can be part of your budget right now.

I know we talked about how getting out of debt helps us lose our taste for spending a lot on extraneous things. Instead, we discover that we really do not need to spend to be happy. This is especially important if you have worked a long time and you are just ready to get out, because you feel like your job is going to kill you. You *can* live on less, but you definitely need to be in a position to do so. By practicing now, you will know if you can do it.

Which Comes First: Paying or Saving?

Is it better to pay off debt first, and then save for retirement? Do both at the same time? Ideally, it would be great to have money in your budget designated for both; however, you are reading a book by someone who, once upon a time, could not afford to order a pizza. I know many of you are strapped, and there is no extra money in your budget.

So here's what I say: yes, it's great if you can tweak your budget until money is landing in both funds—retirement *and* debt reduction. Once your debt is paid off, shift some of that money into retirement and start adding more to your emergency fund. If it is not possible for you to continue with retirement contributions *and* pay down the debt quickly, then you might have to lower or suspend your retirement contributions temporarily until you have reduced your debt. Once your debt is manageable, then resume higher retirement contributions.

But what if you are already contributing to a retirement account, and your employer matches it up to a certain percentage? If you can swing it, stay in, but only up to the matching portion of your employer, so you can double your money and get the magical effect of compounding interest (stay tuned, we will get to that in just a moment).

How much to contribute to retirement comes back to your individual situation. If you have cut out restaurants, gotten cheaper insurance policies, gotten rid of cable, clipped every corner of your spending, and still cannot free up any money, it is time to swallow hard and accept that, temporarily, you need to forgo investing in retirement and knock out some debt. As you tweak your budget each month, look for opportunities to open up and contribute to your retirement again, even if it is only $50 a month.

There will always be emergencies and expenses that have to be paid—medical co-pays, prom dresses, a new roof, a new furnace, home and car repairs, and orthodontist bills. They happen to all of us and can be budgeted for, but they can also rob you of your retirement. Consignment stores are full of prom dresses, and you do not have to have a brand-new vehicle, but you do have to have one that is reliable.

Retirement should be peaceful. It is a season where, after working most of your life, you do not want to be dependent on others. You want to live the way you are accustomed to living without working forever or being a burden to someone else. You want to do and see things in your free time, without having to ask someone else to fund it for you. That kind of life costs money. Many people work part-time as they transition into retirement, and that keeps them self-sufficient.

Fair warning: some employers allow employees to take out low-interest "loans" from their own retirement savings, usually at a rate much lower than a financial institution can offer. They will tell you that you are supposedly paying yourself that interest. Do not do it. These "loans" do not allow you to make increased percentages on your money. For instance, if they offer this arrangement to you at 4 percent, you'd only make 4 percent back. And a lot of times, that money is in the stock market, so by taking this "loan," you are freezing your money. Now you have racked up more debt, and another monthly payment is being sucked directly from your check, beyond your control. If you leave that job, the loan is due immediately. Not a good idea.

Your children will likely be strapped with their own expenses as you enter retirement, which should magnify your desire to be self-sufficient. As you help them go to college and get married, make sure that you are also paying yourself first, in order to prepare for your own retirement. You have to set your retirement, sock it away, and forget it.

The Magic of Compounding Interest

Why am I putting the steam on finding a way to save for retirement? Because of this wonderful thing called compounding interest.

Simply put, compounding interest is the addition of interest to the principal sum of your deposits into your retirement account. When you make a deposit, the interest is calculated on the deposit plus the interest accumulated from previous deposits, kind of like interest-on-interest. It makes a sum of money grow at a much faster rate. Mathematicians can hardly explain it, but it will do magical things with your money if it is left alone long enough, being allowed to grow exponentially.

Your retirement contributions are the only time that you get to pay yourself in life. Remember when I said that your money will always find a way to be spent, regardless of whether you name it or not? It is true. That is why I told you early on that you should be the one telling it where to go. There will always be a need or a want for every cent you bring into the home—cars, clothing, food, college expenses, and so on. Retirement savings is your only chance to see the magic of compounding interest work to your benefit.

The earlier you start saving, the more magical your retirement will be. By retirement age, you may not be able to work longer or take another job to make ends meet. Or you may want to travel and do things for enjoyment. I already said it is a bad plan to count on your children to support you, nor would you want them to. At the same time, do not risk your retirement by putting them through college, or paying crazy prices for the "perfect" wedding dress. You have to find a way to put money away for your tomorrow.

Let's take a look at someone who saves early versus someone who starts saving later in life. Cindy starts investing $2,000 a year from age nineteen to twenty-six, and then stops. Her friend Karen gets inspired by Cindy's tenacity, since they are the same age. Karen starts saving at age twenty-seven, contributing $2,000 a year until age sixty-five.

The Story of Cindy and Karen

Both save $2,000 a year. Cindy starts at age 19 and stops at age 26, while Karen starts at age 27 and stops at age 65.

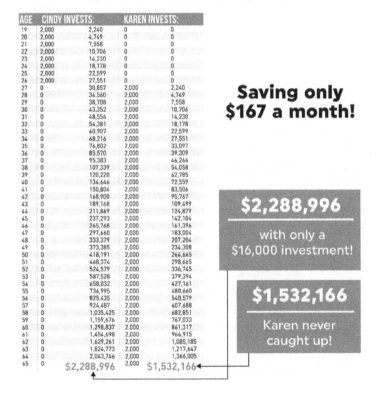

AGE	CINDY INVESTS:		KAREN INVESTS:	
19	2,000	2,240	0	0
20	2,000	4,749	0	0
21	2,000	7,558	0	0
22	2,000	10,706	0	0
23	2,000	14,230	0	0
24	2,000	18,178	0	0
25	2,000	22,599	0	0
26	2,000	27,551	0	0
27	0	30,857	2,000	2,240
28	0	34,560	2,000	4,749
29	0	38,708	2,000	7,558
30	0	43,352	2,000	10,706
31	0	48,554	2,000	14,230
32	0	54,381	2,000	18,178
33	0	60,907	2,000	22,599
34	0	68,216	2,000	27,551
35	0	76,802	2,000	33,097
36	0	85,570	2,000	39,309
37	0	95,383	2,000	46,266
38	0	107,339	2,000	54,058
39	0	120,220	2,000	62,785
40	0	134,646	2,000	72,559
41	0	150,804	2,000	83,506
42	0	168,900	2,000	95,767
43	0	189,168	2,000	109,499
44	0	211,869	2,000	124,879
45	0	237,293	2,000	142,104
46	0	265,768	2,000	161,396
47	0	297,660	2,000	183,004
48	0	333,379	2,000	207,204
49	0	373,385	2,000	234,308
50	0	418,191	2,000	264,665
51	0	468,374	2,000	298,665
52	0	524,579	2,000	336,745
53	0	587,528	2,000	379,394
54	0	658,032	2,000	427,161
55	0	736,995	2,000	480,660
56	0	825,435	2,000	540,579
57	0	924,487	2,000	607,688
58	0	1,035,425	2,000	682,851
59	0	1,159,676	2,000	767,033
60	0	1,298,837	2,000	861,317
61	0	1,454,698	2,000	966,915
62	0	1,629,261	2,000	1,085,185
63	0	1,824,773	2,000	1,217,647
64	0	2,043,746	2,000	1,366,005
65	0	$2,288,996	2,000	$1,532,166

Saving only $167 a month!

$2,288,996
with only a $16,000 investment!

$1,532,166
Karen never caught up!

At the time she stopped, Cindy had contributed a total of $16,000. Karen contributed $2,000 a year for thirty-nine years, and her actual investment totaled $78,000. Meanwhile, Cindy's investment compounds and believe it or not, Karen never catches up with her, even though she saved more money. Getting an early start and benefitting from that compounding interest allows the money to grow exponentially. At a 10 percent return, your money doubles every 7 years. So the moral is if you save less, but early, the benefit is astounding. At age sixty-five, Cindy ends up with $2,288,996. Karen, on the other hand, ends up with $1,532,166, which is still a great amount—but she contributed more for a longer period of time, and Cindy still came out ahead. That is the magic of compounding interest. So, start early and save regularly after you get out of debt. Do not quit. Slow and steady wins the race.

If you get nothing else, get this: *start saving as early as you can for your retirement.*

The idea of compounding interest can't be ignored, even if you do not understand the math. Look at the graph: the earlier you save, the more it grows, and I mean, *a lot* more. If you leave that money alone, it will do things that even the math majors do not truly understand. That is the magic of compounding interest.

Now if you are reading this and feel like you are behind, don't fret, just start saving. *Now.* Some people make very little money and if they live below their means, they can save plenty. In the end, you can do this. It is *never* too late to start saving. Grab some of that peace for yourself; change your future and your family traditions regarding money. It can be done. When you learn to lower your costs and expenses and start saving, it is life-changing!

Trust me, when you have done this for a while—the budgeting, the saving—it will become second nature. You will be able to hit many of your goals and desires without the stress of the debt following you home.

Is There a Percentage Goal?

If we have built up our emergency fund, and have paid off debt, is there a certain percentage of our current income that we should strive to save toward retirement? I say shoot for 15 percent of your income going toward your retirement. This should set you up for a comfortable retirement.

There is a total we can contribute to IRAs each year; the total varies, depending on whether you're age 50 or younger. At age 50, you can add more with catch-up contributions. This total is collective, whether you divide your IRA contributions among a Roth or Traditional. This is not the same type of IRA that you may have through your employer—these limits are for IRAs you have set up yourself, outside of any retirement plans your employer provides.

Once upon a time, employers that offered retirement benefits did so through a pension plan that guaranteed a monthly income for the retiree based on a number of factors and formulas. Pensions were usually a percentage of the retiree's salary, and the trade-off was that employees remained with the company for many years in order to receive the "full" pension.

The government job is one of the few places that still has something like the pension, called FERS (Federal Employee Retirement System). Regardless of what your employer calls your retirement system, learn it and get the full benefit from it. Your future self will thank you.

Today, very few employers offer pensions. Instead, they offer products like 401(k)s and 403(b)s. Employees can designate a percentage of their earnings toward these, sometimes tax-deferred. Many employers will match these contributions up to a certain percentage or dollar amount. If your employer provides this type of retirement plan, start by designating 2 percent of your salary, and any raise you receive after that should go toward retirement. Take advantage of any matching contributions your employer may offer—that's like free money! This doubles your contributions right away. If they match 5 percent, get to that mark of 5 percent as quickly as possible!

If your contributions through work are tax-deferred, you'll be surprised that it will not make as much of a dent in your take-home pay as you think it will. If this money comes out before taxes, you give less tax to Uncle Sam. This translates into more take-home pay. For instance, if you add another $50 per paycheck to your retirement, and that money is taken out before taxes, it might only change your take-home pay by $30. That is the price of a meal at a restaurant. Could you forgo one restaurant meal per pay period, if it meant you would have a nice retirement? It is a more-than-fair trade-off!

If your employer matches up to 5 percent, do what it takes to get there. As soon as possible, set a new goal of 15 percent of your gross income going toward retirement. Fifteen percent is your magic number, the goal of your overall contributions. This may seem impossible to you right now, so start much lower and stay there until you have paid down your debt. Do not leave the matching funds on the table, ever, unless you are working the debt locomotive—but then get right back in!

Employers who offer 401(k)s and 403(b)s do so because they qualify for tax advantages. The primary difference between the two is the type of employer who sponsors the plan—401(k)s are offered by private, for-profit companies, and 403(b)s are only available to employees of nonprofit organizations and government agencies. The contribution limits on these plans are much higher than those you would set up for yourself privately.

These employer-sponsored plans take a lot of the guesswork out of it, but you should still diversify that money, regardless. Do not put all of your contributions into the company's stock, for example. If you do not remember what happened with Enron, I encourage you to look it up. You also need to know what your risk tolerance is and what your options are. Your human resources department should be able to help you there.

And then, there is the question of how much you want to put in stocks versus safer investments. Typically, as you get closer to retirement, you will want to move from a stock-heavy portfolio to bonds or safer options, which will not gain as much but will not lose as much, either. Bonds are considered less risky. Do not rely solely on a quiz or survey to determine your risk tolerance; find someone who is willing to discuss your particular situation, your retirement goals, and how to align them into a retirement plan that works—and keeps up with the cost of living. You will also want to consider when you plan to draw from those funds (within the next five years? Ten years? Twenty?) This makes a difference on how risky you can be with the money. Your money should be in a safer investment the closer you are to withdrawing it. This gains less interest, however, so it is important to have a general idea of when you might like to start your withdrawals.

Regardless of whether your retirement plan is vested with an employer or if you have created your own, it is a good idea to ask an independent fiduciary. This is a very specific type of financial advisor—an investment professional who acts *on behalf of the investor*. When someone is an independent fiduciary, it is his or her legal responsibility to put the interests of the investor before their own. If someone has a fiduciary duty to you, he or she must act solely in your financial interests. Make sure they are fee-for-service, or they offer a free consultation first. Make sure you understand what you are doing. If the advisor cannot explain it in terms that you can understand, find another one.

Gather several options. Eventually, you will need to interview them, and make sure they answer your questions using words that you can understand. Think about whether you could have a trusting working relationship with this person, and find out their certifications.

I asked a money manager, Dean, whom I use personally, to get his take on it. He suggests using the "Three Cs"—character, competency, and chemistry—to gauge a potential investment professional.

Character is probably the hardest to quantify. He says some advisors have no experience at all, but they have great people skills, and unfortunately, these great communicators may also lack character. He recommended visiting brokercheck.finra.org to investigate the compliance record of any licensed financial advisor. For those who are interested in finding a faith-based financial advisor, they can check out kingdomadvisors.com. Or try Dave Ramsey's Endorsed Local Provider (ELP) or SmartVestor programs for additional help in locating a trustworthy investor. You can access these networks online.

Competency is much easier to quantify. My friend advised working only with those who have ten years or more experience as a fiduciary. They need to be a certified financial planner, because that is the gold-standard credential. Ask how many clients they personally assist— if the number is high, keep looking, because they might not have time for you. It is also beneficial if they are part of a team.

Personally, I prefer working with a team rather than a solo advisor. When you work with a team of advisors, you have someone who handles insurance products, another who handles market investments, etc. They all work together.

Finally, consider the *chemistry* between you and the advisor. It is either there, or it is not. Do you think you can get along? Do they do all the talking and very little listening? Plan on narrowing your options to two or three potential advisors before you just settle on one. Interview them. Are they the one for you?

Look at it this way: you pay an independent fiduciary directly, not through commissions, and you are paying them for their advice. It needs to be a teaching relationship, because you need to understand anything that you are investing in. They have to have a teacher's heart. These people can be good people to help you even decide what you're going to do with your employer plan. You just have to find them.

What if you are self-employed, or your employer does not offer a match? Are there special considerations to make? You will likely take out a traditional IRA, a Roth IRA, and/or SEP (simplified employee pension). A big, lingering question with regard to these is: when do you want to pay taxes on this money?

The traditional IRA gives you the option to contribute pre-tax or after-tax, but most usually opt to contribute pre-tax dollars because they can take advantage of the tax benefit now instead of later. Your money grows tax deferred, but your withdrawals will be taxed as current income when you take them out. With a Roth IRA, you contribute after-tax dollars. So your money is already taxed upfront, but all of the money that goes in moving forward is tax-free and you can make tax-free withdrawals after age fifty-nine and a half. So that money grows and even the growth on it will not get taxed later.

There are advantages to both, but here is the short answer if you are undecided which is right for you: With the Roth, you are taxed on the upfront investment, but you do not have to worry about being taxed on this money, or the money it makes for the rest of your life. You can even leave this to your heirs and they will not be taxed on it. With a traditional IRA or 401(k), you deposit the money before taxes, which can be nice, also. You do get taxed on that money, however, when you start taking distributions. The Roth is best suited for an individual who expects to be in a higher tax bracket when he or she starts taking withdrawals, because that money will not be taxed. The traditional is best suited for an individual who expects to be in the same or a lower tax bracket when he or she starts taking withdrawals. In a Roth, your contributions grow tax-free; with the traditional IRA, your taxes are deferred, and you receive an immediate tax benefit.

If you do not make much money, you still need to learn to put money away for retirement, even if it is only $50 a month. Break it down to $10 to $15 each week if you have to; that is less than what you pay for fancy coffee each day. Are you willing to make coffee at home now, so you can enjoy retirement later? Pay your retirement, just like a bill. Pay yourself first.

Turning fifty this year? You have the opportunity to participate in "catch-up contributions." You do not have to wait until your fiftieth birthday; you can start during the calendar year that you turn fifty.

With catch-up contributions, you can currently add up to $6,500 more annually to an employer retirement plan. That's in addition to the $19,500 maximum you are allowed in 2022. You have to reach that first before you can add the catch-up contributions.

If that seems way out of reach, there are a few things you can do to hit those goals. First, focus on reducing your bills to be as small as you can; see if your utility providers offer budget billing, like we discussed back in Chapter 4. This will help you stick to your budget. If you are an empty-nester, maybe it is time to downsize into a home that is much cheaper, smaller, and probably has cheaper utility bills. Maybe you are not attached to your geographic location and you could move to a cheaper state (some states do not tax your retirement income, and others do not have a state income tax). Some people just rent for the rest of their lives, because then they do not pay property taxes and are not responsible for the costs associated with home ownership. Consider buying and moving into a duplex. You could live on one side and rent the other for extra income.

These are just a few ideas to help you clear the way for catch-up contributions.

What About Reverse Mortgages?

Let's talk about reverse mortgages for a moment. I see them advertised all the time and they make it seem so simple and low-risk. A lot of people kind of get roped into them, and get taken. Is it obvious I am not a big fan of reverse mortgages?

A reverse mortgage is a special type of home loan only for home-owners who are sixty-two and older. You are borrowing money, using your home as security for the loan. When you take out a reverse-mortgage loan, the title to your home remains in your name. Your home must already be paid off, and the company sends you monthly checks.

The loan is repaid when the borrower no longer lives in the home. Additional interest and fees are added to the loan balance each month, and the balance grows.

Homeowners are still required to pay their property taxes and homeowners insurance, and keep the house in good condition. A reverse mortgage loan is not free money; it is a loan with borrowed money, plus interest and fees. Each month equals a rising loan balance. The homeowners or their heirs will eventually have to pay back this loan. That usually requires selling the house after your death to pay this loan.

Some people can't make ends meet and resort to a reverse mortgage for this reason. Between the added fees and interest, that should be enough to scare anyone away from them—but these companies hire favorite actors to extol the "benefits" of a reverse mortgage, and people trust them not to lie. These actors are paid, just like any other job. If they are being paid to pretend they're trustworthy, they deliver. If they are paid to be a TV villain, they deliver. If they are pretending that reverse mortgages have merit, they are being paid to be a wolf in sheep's clothing.

The small glimmer of hope is that, if you signed to secure one, you have three days to change your mind, but it has to be in writing. If you have signed for a reverse mortgage and want out before three days pass, overnight the letter, get a return receipt, leave no stone unturned to create a paper trail that proves you canceled this transaction in writing within three days. After that point, you may be stuck with it. You will have to talk to a lawyer to see what your options are.

If you are in such a desperate place that you are considering a reverse mortgage, consider some alternatives instead. Have a friend or relative move in, let them pay some rent and help with the bills. Downsize yourself into a smaller home or apartment. Lastly, sell your house by yourself and find a cheaper place to live or rent. I would think about these things before taking out a reverse mortgage.

Other Retirement 'Eaters'

I have briefly mentioned a few items that tend to eat our retirement, and for some of you, these may seem harsh to cut out of your budget. You may feel as though it makes you a bad parent, for example, to not pay for your child's college education or make their car payments for them, or fund your daughter's dream wedding.

Your retirement is much more important than funding your children's college. You only have this one chance to get the compounding interest, and you need to take it. Your children will not be able to support you in retirement; it is not unheard of that they pay for, or assist in paying for, their own college costs.

- They can live with you and attend a community college that is within driving distance.

- They can also drive back and forth to a larger state college, especially if within a one-hour radius.

- They can apply for scholarships, grants, and other financial aid in a variety of places.

If they are footing even a portion of the bill, they will value their education even more. It's not that I do not value education; quite the opposite, actually. I have two advanced degrees of my own, and here I am, getting ready to jump back into my third, but I also believe that there are cheaper ways to get a good, quality education. Every avenue should be explored, especially at this time in our country.

Some may argue that a college education does not get you very far. I still believe that a college degree advances you in any career path you choose, although you may be initially competing for jobs that previously required only a high school education.

I have seen many kids leave college with a degree and $40,000 to $50,000 in debt and no promise of a job. Many have not had direction in exploring their gifts and the different career fields that lend themselves to these gifts and passions. There is free testing offered in most high schools and college settings, and even online to help anyone—a teenager, middle-ager, even a senior—explore careers that would complement his or her personality. Another area that often gets overlooked is trade school. We all know how hard it is to find someone who can do quality plumbing, electrical, or construction. Sometimes these "dirty" jobs are overlooked by young kids who think that an office job signals success. Trust me, quality service providers are earning a really good living!

These careers may not seem prestigious, but they can provide well for a family and are fairly secure. Your children need direction and lots of opportunities to explore different career paths without actually entering the career. Parents can help their children find these opportunities through job shadowing, conversation, or even local career fairs. Thanks to the internet, they can gather information on hard-to-find niche jobs and what qualifications could give them a leg up.

These are great ways to help your children in all aspects of their lives. Do not leverage your retirement to send your children to college. If you have already done this, you must work longer to get yourself and your future back on track. You can do it!

Now let's talk about car payments. Research shows that most millionaires buy good used cars and let someone else take the financial hit on new vehicles. They also shop at retail outlets and live in the first home that they bought. Even Warren Buffett, one of the richest men in the world, still lives in the same house that he bought in 1963. Many times what we *think* rich people do is not what they do at all. We do not always have to have a car payment. And when you have more than one car payment, it puts a tight squeeze on the budget and the needs of the family.

Brad and I have been able to afford those extra expenses and put more in our retirement over the years because we only had one reasonable car payment at a time. Once a vehicle is paid off, we start plugging that money into a car fund for next time. This system allows us to afford big down payments on future cars and sometimes pay cash for it outright. Do not let the smell of new-car leather cause you to have to work a lot longer at a job that you do not even enjoy, or keep you from retiring at all. If you stick to this plan, there will be a day when you can buy a new car outright—if that is what you want to do with your money. Until then, keep the cars that you have in good working condition. Be a good steward with what you already own.

Remember that old van of mine with the broken door? I already mentioned that I cleaned it out each week, and I steam-cleaned it at least once a year. I had four kids, their friends, sports equipment, all their eating and drinking inside that van. When colleagues went with me to lunch, they could not believe my van was as old as it was. When you take care of your vehicle and keep it clean, even if it is an old minivan, you will not mind driving it as much.

This brings me to another "retirement eater." Do not sit around thinking that you're going to be happy when you get to a certain income level, or have saved up a certain amount of money. A *Time* magazine article in 2010 details research from Princeton University in which it was found that day-to-day happiness does not increase above $75,000 yearly income. That is the amount where most can pay their bills and have some expendable income for fun. Our happiness levels do not increase by making more money. Think about that for a minute.

Be happy *now*, for every day that you have; be grateful for breath and for life itself. Do not miss out on your life because you think it doesn't start unless you have hit a particular financial threshold. Realize your life matters now, so that you find happiness and contentment outside of your finances.

We have learned during the COVID pandemic that we must enjoy today, because it could look very different tomorrow. The pandemic has also taught us that there might not be a tomorrow.

So whatever happened to Bart and Lori? Well, they decided to forgo some vacations they had planned to take in their final year of working, decided to work one year longer, and plug away hard at the debt. This strategy allowed them to enter retirement with no debt, beyond one small car payment. Their stress relief was palpable. The year they retired, the entire family took a paid-for Disney cruise, and every photo was brimming with smiles, especially theirs.

We all hope to reach retirement age, so we have to prepare starting now, wherever "now" is for you. Do you want a good retirement, or a great one? It is never too early or too late to start planning for retirement—money does its magic when you start early and leave it alone. You can have a great life now, and a great retirement later.

Discipline and consistency are key. Live differently from everyone else *now* so that later, you can live differently. You will be able to have peace in your finances and buy what you want with cash. You will be able to live the life you want and help others along the way. Your life will be better than 90 percent of the population. Are you ready to join the other 10 percent? Are you sure?

WANNA HAVE FUND$?

See if your company has a retirement plan, and if it doesn't, find one and earmark $50 a month in your budget that deposits directly into it.

CHAPTER 7

How Bad Do You Want It?

I have always been intrigued with money, even from a young age. I liked to build it up in my piggy bank. And then later, I put it in a regular bank. I did not really want to spend my money as a young child, but one thing that I would spend my money on was Richie Rich comic books. You might say he was my first mentor.

The comic book covers were really bright and vivid. He had so much money that even his middle name was $, a dollar sign. Richie had great big eyes and looked so friendly. He was smart, clever, happy, and generous. He was the son of a wealthy businessman. He had a dog named Dollar. He had his own chef, a robot maid, a butler, and even a personal scientist called Professor Keenbean. This may sound odd, but I can still feel the relief I had when I read those books—in spite of all his wealth, Richie Rich was down to earth and someone I could be friends with.

Most of the plots centered on people trying to steal the Rich family's wealth, and it was up to Richie to figure out what was going on. Of course, what stood out in my mind as a young child was the bright, shiny covers and colorful pages full of money, jewels, and every contraption a kid could want, like snow cone machines, carnivals, and limos, but even better than reality's versions. Richie was so very generous with it all. He shared everything with his friends and looked out for the underdog, always. I do not know if he taught me to feel the same way, but looking out for the underdog has always been on my radar. He looked out for the needy, and this is what I knew I wanted to do, even during some of my leanest financial years. You do not have to wait until you have a lot of money before you are generous. I firmly believe that if you keep your money on a flat hand, money can come and go as the universe needs. And if you hang onto it with a tight fist, you may keep what you have, but more cannot come in. There may have been much more that needed to come in, but if you are not a good steward and you're hoarding it for yourself, this will get you nowhere—and you will feel scared when you think about money. By the same token, money can slip away if your hand is loose and not supporting it with a reasonable, manageable budget.

When I started writing this book, I was over the moon to discover that my sweet mother kept a box full of my old Richie Rich comic books for me all these years. I look at the now-faded covers and still feel a weird sense of peace, almost a reinforcement of my desire to help people.

I do not think that Richie taught me to love money, but he showed me something that I had never really seen: a world where people had everything they wanted. I did not have any sort of wealth like that. Certainly, I had what I needed, but I could not get what I *wanted*.

Now to be clear, I do not think I suffered over it, but Richie's world caught my eye. I held jobs at an early age, and I did not care how hard they were. For example, I detassled corn many summers, and I ran a concession stand in a local movie theater while I was still in middle school. I searched for jobs like that, and it was kind of unheard of. When people found out I was running the concession stand, they were a little surprised.

I got my first checkbook in middle school and used it to buy my own school clothes. When my cousins came to visit, we would go to a restaurant and I would write a check for our pizza. I can remember getting a strange look from the business owner, but I didn't care, because I knew I had money in there.

The truth is, I love numbers and at one point considered becoming a math teacher, until my favorite math teacher, Samuel T. Patton, told me that there was not much money in it and he only did it to get health insurance, since he was a farmer. Then I thought I might become a CPA, but medicine caught my eye and took the reins. Even so, I never forgot about Richie Rich and his giving heart.

We All Have Something to Give

There is an old adage about generosity—"the more you give, the more you receive"—and it is true. Even if you try to fly under the radar to remain anonymous, someone is going to tell someone else about your generosity. When Jesus healed the sick, he would often tell people to keep it to themselves, and they just couldn't. We do not give for the recognition—in fact, recognition can get kind of embarrassing—but giving gives you a type of peace that reaches beyond anything money can buy. You always get more than you give!

It is a similar peace that comes from working hard. When we have worked hard to attain a goal, particularly a goal that can be expanded and shared through generosity, the payoff goes beyond anything that can be found in a bank account. Our society is one of instant gratification—just like microwaves provide us a shortcut to a hot meal, we often want "microwaved" answers delivered to our problems instead of working hard and diligently finding them ourselves.

The habit of working hard for years to achieve or earn can seem too far in the future to pay off. We have been programmed to see if we can afford the monthly payment instead of the total cost, including interest. We can change the way we think—it is possible to see a different way.

This is, in part, why the four steps encourage quick, massive action—to see successes along the way. This propels you more quickly on your pathway to financial freedom. Your life will change in eighteen to twenty-four months. Some do it sooner, as they get busy taking care of business. The benefits you receive by waiting and earning what you want are immense. Your character grows with each step. When you achieve your goals, there is real joy, but you also feel tremendous satisfaction throughout the journey.

Think of the last time you financed something, either by a loan or credit card, that you really wanted. How long did the happiness last? Probably not very long. The transaction lacked the perseverance and hard work it takes to buy something outright. You missed out on what builds character, competence, and long-term happiness.

As you are working through the four steps, you do not want to wish away the next two years of learning to manage finances. We want to be present, relish the memories we make, and give generously when we can. Learn and grow all that you can. As you commit to the four steps, enjoy the journey and live each moment to the fullest.

One of my favorite teachers, Samuel T. Patton (STP), used to tell me to be willing to burn the midnight oil. He even called me into his office after I had my baby in high school.

"I'm not a rich man, Monica, but you are smart, and you need to go to college," he said. "If you get accepted into college and find out that you can't make it financially, you look me up." Thankfully, I never had to ask him for financial assistance, but his promise meant a lot to me at the time. This also reinforced the idea that one does not have to be rich to be generous.

Between Richie Rich, my own mother, and STP, I realized that generosity does not begin with great wealth, but great wealth can certainly enable greater generosity. I determined I would help people, and as my wealth increased, so would my generosity. I visualized what that would look like from a young age and at different points throughout my life.

Reprogram Your Subconscious

Visualization is not just seeing something in your mind while your eyes are closed. It is not just the formation of a mental image of something. Visualization lives in the space where you have called it to exist, and you have faith that it does and will exist. There is enormous power in mental visualization that can be used for positive things. Our world was birthed out of God's thought and vision, and while I am not suggesting that we are on the same level as God, I am saying that he cast the original vision. He gave us the ability and showed us how to visualize. As you work through my four-step plan, visualize what financial freedom looks like in your house, your community, your world.

When we visualize, we also tap into our subconscious. We do not think much about this because, well, it is our subconscious. Our daily routines, disciplines, and habits are just programmed in. I mean, when was the last time you had to put much thought into brushing your teeth, taking a shower, driving to work, or even breathing? You can actually live a large portion of your life just in the subconscious. In his book, *The Biology of Belief*, Bruce Lipton details his epigenetic research on the power of the subconscious. The subconscious mind controls 90 percent of our lives when we are awake.

Think about some of the tasks you perform on autopilot. Many times we bring ourselves back around to consciousness, but then we will flip back into the programs of our subconscious mind very quickly.

Dr. Lipton has conducted research on individual cells and the brain, showing how we can reprogram our subconscious during lower activity right before sleep and upon awakening. He believes this reprogramming is when we will realize that we can have what we ask for. This is an oversimplification, but hang in here with me for a minute.

The subconscious mind is mainly formed before we are six to seven years old. The memories, both conscious and subconscious, that reside there are what forms you, but you do not get to pick what happens before you are six or seven. Think back to some early incidents that you can remember. Perhaps you acted badly at a store, and you were told you did not deserve a particular toy. Maybe you experienced long periods of hurt or isolation. I do not want to blame our families for anything that we went through, or hold them responsible for whatever lingers in our subconscious, whether they are right, wrong, or even accurately recalled. Regardless, these incidents may have triggered our subconscious mind to behave in certain ways and expect certain things. I do not want to go too deeply here, beyond saying that we possess the power to change, and to reprogram our minds through visualization.

How is it done? Usually, it happens during the first hour before going to sleep and during the first thirty minutes after you wake up. These periods are known as *theta*, and theta is really the only time you can reprogram your subconscious. Visualizations are designed to reprogram the mind, and you may find some apps to use that can help you.

Is visualization the same thing as positive thinking? Well, let me ask you this: Have you ever read a self-help book, or gone to a seminar and thought it was great? Later, did you really change, or was the change only temporary until real life took over again?

It is the subconscious—our auto-drive—that has to be changed. It goes deeper than positive thinking, which is why I recommend using mental visualization during theta, right before going to bed and right when you wake up. You simply reprogram your mind and let it do the work for you. We say positive things to and about ourselves, visualize it, and feel that they have already happened. You can also reprogram it by doing actions over and over again to develop good habits, or making different choices. This is where these different financial choices are going to change you.

Likewise, the people we are connected to can bring out positive and negative emotions in us. This is something we have control over. So do your best to limit the negative, particularly when we recognize the effect someone has on our thoughts and judgments. These thoughts control a large part of your destiny. If you think negative thoughts about someone, they say that there is a reciprocal effect: they feel your negative energy and it flows back to you. Nothing even has to be spoken. This can be disruptive to what you want out of life, and gives us a good reason to stay positive, even with our thoughts.

There is an old saying that if you pray for someone you are mad at, you can't be mad at them anymore. It is so true. Positivity yields positivity. Negativity only hurts you.

If you have not read Napoleon Hill's book *Think and Grow Rich*, I highly recommend it. For the book, originally written in 1937, he interviewed five hundred wealthy people and recorded their reflections on life. What makes it especially interesting was the fact that they had lived through the Great Depression but still ended up just fine. Hill's conclusion was that whatever your mind concentrates on is what you will become.

I carry around a card that says, "I am a best-selling author on women and money management." I read this twice a day and it helps me keep my eyes on the goal. Staying focused reinforces my own visualization of success, that I want to help as many people as I can along this journey. So yes, think about your financial success, but you must also *visualize* and internalize it, as though it has already happened to you. This is an important step because if you can truly believe it has already happened (and it will), then you can have the peace and joy that comes along with it right now. It is not easy, at least at first, but you can ask the universe for anything. We all have a purpose to fulfill, when we are ready. Some never are. Are you?

Excuses Won't Get You There

Stop thinking of reasons why you can't be successful and financially secure. Act the part of your already successful self. If you are really doing this to the fullest, then you are actually feeling like you are already financially healthy. This kind of hope gives you a brighter outlook, and in turn, attracts positive vibration. You are going to feel great, and others are going to feel great just being around you.

One of the people Napoleon Hill interviewed was a man who wanted to be partners with Thomas Edison. He *knew* he would make an excellent partner, but he could not afford to travel to see him. He bummed a ride on a cargo train and arrived at Edison's workshop, all disheveled. He told him, "I will work for you and become your partner." Edison was taken aback by this guy's appearance but liked his confidence, so he hired him to work around the shop. For five years, this guy did menial tasks to the best of his ability and with a great attitude, knowing he would be ready for the partnership later.

Edison's sales representatives hated the idea of his Victor phonograph contraption. They did not think it would sell, nor did they even want to attempt to sell it. This guy stepped up and said, "I can sell it, and I will." And he did! Edison's phonograph ended up being a revolutionary invention, and a successful partnership was created between a "nobody" with his own inner vision of success and America's greatest inventor. Some may say it was just a lucky break, but the traveler knew he was supposed to be Edison's partner. He felt it, he lived it, and he made it happen. It was not empty hope; it was a pulsating desire that transcended all else. And that is the power of visualization.

So here are six steps to harness your own power of visualization:

1.   Fix in your mind exactly what you desire. Getting out of debt? Financial independence?

2.   Determine exactly what you intend to give in return for this accomplishment, and make sure hard work is part of it.

3. Establish a definite date when you intend for this to happen. One year? Two years? I recommend massive, quick action or you may lose heart and give up.

4. Create a definite plan for carrying out your desire, whether you are ready or not, and put the plan into action.

5. Write a clear, concise statement that names the desire, the time limit, and what you will give in return, and describes your plan clearly.

6. Read the statement aloud twice daily, when you wake up in the morning and before you go to bed at night. See, feel, and believe yourself financially free already.

One of my favorite sayings is: "Fake it 'til you make it." That is the bottom line of your visualization: feel what you want and act like you are already there. In time it will become a reality. If you decide you are going to do these four steps, you need to know it, feel it, live it, and make it happen. It does require work, so visualization is not a passive exercise. This is not some "name it to claim it" notion. You have to want it badly enough to put the four steps into action.

Author Wayne Dyer says, "If you change the way you look at things, then the things you look at change." Albert Einstein said, "Whether you look at the universe as hostile or loving, the problem is inside—but you are looking outside for the answer. I believe that it will be what you think it is." You can fail at doing what you do not want to do, so why not succeed at doing what you love to do?

Keep your focus on the end point, but move step-by-step, day by day. Try to enjoy this journey, because you are still living your life along the way. True enjoyment is found on the journey. It is the process. Few people stay exhilarated when they finish a goal. The pinnacle of success is sweet but does not last that long before most people look ahead and make a new goal. Enjoy the process, and who you are becoming along the way!

There is a different level of consciousness at theta that helps you imprint this reality on your brain. I believe that the positive ideas you concentrate on before falling into slumber are the ones that impress on your subconscious the most. So, if you imprint good ideas, your subconscious mind will take over for the time you are sleeping. Why not implant your goals in your mind? This can be life-changing for your attitude, and you will find that you have energy available to work on your goals. Your subconscious mind can actually do some of the work in getting to your goals more quickly.

The blessings you receive as you strive to be a good steward are endless. When you are incorporating good money management skills with a keen desire to do better in life, you can't help but succeed. This will enable you to think up new ideas and insights that others may not. You are feeding your mind with good, healthy things. You are working hard with what you have. This is when the magic happens. You will move through the four steps while visualizing the outcome. Goals are the main key to get these things done. If you put effort into your goals, along with positive thoughts and hard work, it will pay off and you will achieve them.

While everyone else seems content with the status quo, your life will change. A person's life is what their own thoughts make of it. Think and believe that you are already debt-free. You will feel this is already true, all the way to financial independence. As the writer Ralph Waldo Emerson said, "A man is what he thinks about all day long." If you compare the human mind with farmland, you grow what you plant in it. Positive or negative, we become what we plant in our minds, and the human mind is fertile soil. Plant in your mind all that is happy, goal-oriented, kind, compassionate, generous, loving, and prosperous. Everything of real value was given to us freely—our minds, souls, ambitions, and dreams. These are not only free, but also the only things we take with us. Value and use these free gifts to their fullest.

When Financial Freedom Is in Focus

What does financial freedom actually look like? Too often, we catch fleeting glimpses, but we really do not have a focused picture in mind. When we dare ourselves to try to get a clear visual, we might start out thinking about spending—but please focus on your end goal instead: financial freedom.

When the bills are paid, the retirement plan is humming, the mortgage is shrinking, and you do not fear tomorrow, financial freedom is within your grasp. When you have memorized every detail of your child's face because your mind is not worrying about how to pay the power bill, financial freedom is coming in clearer. When you sleep better at night because you have not had another argument with your partner about the credit card bill, financial freedom is crisp and clear. When you wake up in the morning, excited to embrace the day and take a moment to breathe in and out with gratitude, knowing that you are not in the same financial place you were last month or last year, you are living the journey of financial freedom.

Financial freedom is not about spending. Its value is far more intrinsic. It is more priceless than gold.

Do not just hold your breath for the next eighteen to twenty-four months and hope it all works out. How you *feel* about things really matters. Be careful which feelings receive your time and energy, because feelings can trick you. If you feel negative or sad when you wake up, but do not know why, redirect yourself. Pay attention, and direct your thoughts in a positive manner.

We cannot achieve anything without paying a price. You have to be willing to put forth a certain amount of effort in order to achieve anything. So what is the price? You have to understand, emotionally and intellectually, that there is work involved as you learn to control your thoughts. Set clear, defined goals, and think positively about them. Let your mind explore your goals from all different angles and find different possible solutions. Act promptly. When the course is clear, do not sit around thinking about it or mulling over it for years; make a plan and stick to it. You have to act on it.

You are standing in your own solution. Use it. Good ideas are worthless unless we are willing to act on them. You have the information to change your household's financial future. Will you do it?

Know Your Worth

Look at the abundance that surrounds you. There may be a voice deep inside you that whispers, *You are being selfish, you don't deserve this.* I want to address that voice directly. If you strive for what you want, you are not taking it from someone else. There is plenty in the universe for everyone.

Women are especially vulnerable to undervaluing themselves. We worry so much about what others think, and we have to make everything perfect for everybody. We devalue ourselves regarding what we deserve and need to do for us. We devalue our own feelings and put everyone before ourselves, wanting to make their lives perfect. Hear me on this: *It is totally impossible to make everything perfect for everyone all of the time. I guarantee that someone is going to be unhappy despite your efforts.*

We do not think highly of ourselves, comparing our lives to others who profile and filter their lives on social media. We are so used to multitasking and doing things for free, we do not even consider these as skills that deserve compensation. We do not document or take credit for what we have done in our jobs. Instead, we let other people tell us what we are worth.

You have skills that you are likely using that help others and you do not even give yourself credit for. We do not negotiate or outright ask to be paid for what our skills are worth. In some cultures, that is considered "tacky," and in religious or nonprofit circles, you might be expected to take low or no compensation. Some believe that money is the root of evil and they must do things *only* to store up treasure in heaven. Let me be clear, it is the *love* of money that is evil. When you love money, you use it only for your selfish desires and are not generous. We deserve to earn competitive pay for what we do.

In my own experience, I see many pastors' wives who run into this problem. Depending on the size and stability of the congregation, pastors' salaries are a broad range. Some pastors have second and third jobs, while some do quite well. Their wives are in particularly precarious situations, because they are expected to serve alongside their husbands, plus coordinate various events, serve on committees, teach, actively participate in the community, and so on, without receiving any sort of stipend or salary. It is somehow considered their "duty." If someone is happy doing this and does not need or want compensation for their time, then fine, but if they are not living a similar standard of living when compared to the congregation, it might be a problem.

Am I saying we should not volunteer or donate our time? Absolutely not! In fact, particularly when we are paying off debt and getting our finances together, time is one thing we are able to donate. The time donation can mean the most as research shows about 10% of the people are doing the majority of the donated work.

Let's start with your full-time job. In those situations, you are contracted to a specific job description and have agreed to compensation in exchange for job performance. Now, many job descriptions will end with the sly and mysterious "other duties as assigned," a catchall phrase in the event they need extra work out of you, or ask you to absorb another person's responsibilities. They play the "other duties" card a lot during reorganizations and downsizing, and we feel threatened if we do not just go along to get along. If you're trying to get your finances in order, this threat can add even more stress because you need that paycheck to make it work.

If this is happening to you, keep careful records. Document everything you are doing and sharpen your skill sets and marketability. Always keep your eyes open for new opportunities. With another job offer on the table, you have some room for negotiation. If they are not going to pay you for what you are doing, particularly if you have absorbed another person's role and you are overworked, then you need to have a serious discussion, but you do not want to go into it empty-handed. You want to go in with documentation, and in the meantime, get all the experience you can. One of two things will happen: your current employer will work with you to either reduce your workload or pay you more, *or* you will take the other opportunity that has been offered to you. Do not go into this angry or looking for a fight; stay cool, keep your composure and dignity, and give your current employer the opportunity to right the wrong. If they do not see it the way you do, they may not value what you are bringing to the table. Aside from all of this, doing your job well yet keeping your eyes open for promotions or different jobs will only help you get your budget in order more quickly. I think employers will see your efforts and compensate you accordingly. Those are the ones who get promoted within the agency.

Volunteering is unpaid time working to the benefit of others or the community as a whole. There are no employment contracts for volunteer work, though it can sometimes lead to employment, either with the organization or through contacts you make while volunteering. In those cases, you get a trial run to show how valuable you are and whether you enjoy working with them. Plus, you are contributing to something you are passionate about. That is the good side of volunteerism. What is the downside?

The time and effort you are putting in might be disproportionate to what others are supposed to be putting in. Or you are putting in full-time hours when they really need to hire staff.

Stay-at-home mothers, be especially alert: if you are organizing charity events or other types of fundraisers and assigned staff are not putting in at least the same amount of time, if not more, this needs to be addressed. You are managing a major project, setting up committees, going to meetings, maintaining a budget, handling logistics—skills that people get paid for. The caterer you are hiring is not likely to donate their services and food; they may discount it, but they are not doing it for free. The staff member assigned to the event draws a salary too. Be very careful about what you are being asked to do for free, particularly if you are in the process of working the four steps. Make sure there are rewards and benefits to your participation (even if it is barter or trade) or that there are plenty of other volunteers to delegate, and therefore reduce the amount of time you are putting in. Otherwise, that gut feeling turns to resentment and burnout. Women struggle in this area.

Whether you are married or single, you need to provide. You have to put food on your table. Many times, the increase in responsibilities is so gradual, supervisors do not realize they are burning out their best employees until it is too late. The same is true for nonprofits and churches; the organizers may be super-wealthy and do not have to work, so they just figure everyone has the same luxury of donating the same amount of time. Give them the chance to right the ship; at least that way, you can walk away with an eased conscience that you gave them the opportunity.

Also consider your level of experience. When I was younger, I was much more willing to be a "Jill of all trades," and as a result, I know a little bit about everything in medicine. When COVID hit, I was in high demand. My oath and integrity kicked in, so I rallied, but it was intense. I saw many colleagues give up, exhausted—and in full transparency, I was almost one of them. As of this writing, providers are at a premium because so many are burned out. When someone is spent, they cannot pursue dreams. When you are spent, you are too exhausted to even attempt to dream, much less pursue them. Know your value, and make this factor into your dream of financial freedom.

Do You Love Money?

I am a person of faith, so I speak to a lot of women's groups and churches about finances. My coaching, however, is not limited to people of faith or churches; sometimes, I am working with individuals, couples, and organizations who are simply passionate about a particular cause or the work they do. Regardless, when we talk about knowing our own worth, the conversation can get a little uncomfortable. I am not going to start quoting scripture, but I know some of you might be reading this and thinking, *She might be a little money-hungry*. You may be worried that if you work these four steps, people may accuse you of the same.

To that I say, we are not called to be poor; we are called to be generous. The love of money can be defined as an intense and selfish desire to get more money, willingness to do anything for the sake of money without considering the morality or consequences of it. When you love money in that way, you will do anything to achieve material gain. That is not what I am about, nor are the four steps.

The Bible says that the *love* of money is the root of all evil. It does not say that just by virtue of *having* money, that is the root of all evil. It is not money itself, but the *worship* of it that is the problem. When we put money first—before God and our relationships—no good can come of it.

On the other hand, there are many good, wealthy people who love God, their families, and their communities. They put the importance of these things before money and before the acquisition of more money. Many people have budgeted their money, gotten out of debt, and (in gratitude) use that wealth to be generous to others and to good causes. These are the people who help others who are in need.

So it is a good thing for society to have good people with money. They will be actively involved and with an open hand. In this way, money comes in and goes out as needed. Resources are allowed to flow freely, as opposed to clinging with a tight fist, or flippantly wasting or boastfully throwing it around.

If anything, money magnifies who you truly are. Truly generous people have held this open hand from the beginning—while they were starting out, budgeting, saving, and building. If you have been generous and kind-spirited all along, you will be more of the same, and vice versa, regardless of what you currently have in the bank.

I recently came upon a new word: *avaricious*. It is defined as having, or showing, an extreme greed for wealth or material gain—exactly what society does *not* need. What we need is more generosity. When you get your financial house in order, it frees you to cultivate more generosity in your life as well.

There is a reason flight attendants instruct us to place our own oxygen masks on before we assist others. If you are a mother, your instinct will be to put the mask on your child, but if you lose consciousness in the process, you both may die. By getting your own house in order first—that is, becoming financially free—what you do, and how you manage what you have, makes you a greater blessing to help others.

So if you want to be who you are truly meant to be, you have to get your own finances in order. You are still searching, and you want something different. You do not want to live the way the rest of the country is living—paycheck-to-paycheck, or paycheck-to-credit card. At your very core, you know that joy and peace are what your heart desires. You want to create and leave a legacy that others can benefit from and expand its footprint. Put on the oxygen mask.

I'm no Bible scholar, but I love the Sermon on the Mount. It says for us to ask and it shall be given; seek, and you shall find; knock and the door will be opened. You know what you need to do now; it is time for you to be a good steward and do it. The blessings will flow beyond your wildest dreams. It is so marvelous, yet so simple.

You can work the four steps with calm reassurance, do your job as never before, be the best employee ever, keeping your eyes open for new opportunities that will reveal themselves to you when it is time. Think in terms of every contact presenting an opportunity to impress, to learn, or get promoted.

We earn money by providing things to others that are necessary and useful. We expect that our financial return will be in direct proportion to our service. Making money is the result of our success, not the other way around. It is like telling a stove to give you some heat without putting wood in it first. We have to put the fuel in before we get the heat. You will not be financially secure without enriching others. You may make money, but it doesn't compare to the peace that comes from reaching back to help others. That is priceless.

The four-step plan is simple. Stop worrying, stop procrastinating, and just get started. This is your time.

WANNA HAVE FUND$?

Visualize one dream. Write it out, or put it in pictures on a storyboard and keep it somewhere that you will see it often. Each week, add one action you have taken to realize this dream.

CHAPTER 8

Stop Wasting Time!

I HAVE CONSIDERED MYSELF A RUNNER FOR MANY YEARS NOW. WHAT started out as power walking at lunch transitioned, following a job change where I did not have as much flexibility during that hour. As a result, my exercise significantly decreased, because my four kids had a lot of sporting events right after work that would last until late in the evening.

One morning while walking into work, I saw my friend Audrey running from her car, headed into work. For the next several days, I noticed her doing this.

"Are you always running late?" I called out to her.

"No. I just like to make sure that I can still run," she replied.

What the heck in the world? I thought. (If you and I ever meet in person, that is one of my signature phrases, borrowed from my five-year-old granddaughter, Madi.)

Audrey was a few years older than me, so she got me thinking. Could I run? So I started finding out, walk-running first before graduating to full-on running. When I could go nonstop for three miles, I got hooked on the runner's high; it felt like I had taken an antidepressant. I felt young again! To me, it is the best antidepressant there is, so I had to start getting up early to get the exercise in.

I started an informal survey with my patients, asking them about their exercise habits (particularly because there are many benefits to it). Many of them did not exercise but planned to do so when they retired. But you know, right now, their lives were too busy, work was too stressful; the reasons were fairly common. As the years wore on and some of these same patients retired, they never started an exercise regimen. My conclusion is that what you find important before retirement will most likely be what is important after retirement. You make time for what is important to you.

This is part of the reason I make myself exercise, whether I feel like it or not. I find running partners to hold me accountable. You get each other up, even on frosty mornings, and get it done. I am often asked, *How do you do it? I can't get up that early, before daylight.*

For starters, I prepare myself and my mind before I go to bed—laying out exercise clothes, setting the alarm, and going to bed at a decent time. Next, I no longer hit "snooze." I say, *3, 2, 1...Boom!* Like fireworks. I hit the alarm button to turn it off, and get right up. I tune out any tired thoughts drawing me back to sleep. Instead, I think about how good I will feel after the exercise is over. I consider my running partner, who is meeting me and counting on me to be there. (Special shoutout to Holly, my faithful, tried, and true running buddy—we've been "running the town" for many years!)

While others are lying warm and cozy in their beds, Holly and I know that we are in the top percentage of people who continue to exercise regularly, and that it pays off. We've made discoveries, and saved lives... well almost, like the time we discovered a large trashcan fire and a gas leak. We even stopped a crime that was about to happen (or so we thought—it was actually a new employee on his early-morning paper route). We look younger and we definitely feel younger than others our age. I believe it is because of this regular exercise.

It didn't happen overnight; the plan, the process, and the persistence got me to that payoff. Once I got there, I *wanted* to keep going in order to maintain that feeling and possibly exceed any current goals I had set for myself.

Speed Up the Process

What you are doing today decides where you will be ninety days from now, so you need to stop wasting time and decide what you want. Start making those small, manageable steps toward your goals. This is the only way to change your ninety-day trajectory. You can sit and procrastinate and think of all the reasons why you do not want to, or why you just can't get started. Instead, why not just get started on your financial plan?

The quicker you start, the quicker you will reach your goals. Do not pay attention to the thoughts that try to talk you out of it—know what you want, and go for it. In the last chapter, we devoted a great deal of time to visualization and getting clarity on what you really want. Think about how you are going to feel and where you will be mentally and emotionally when it is done. Begin to see the benefits that financial freedom and peace of mind will bring.

If it sounds overwhelming, let me share some encouragement from world-renowned motivational speaker Tony Robbins. He suggests asking yourself three simple questions to propel yourself forward faster:

- What do I really want?
- What is my purpose?
- What do I need to do *now*?

When you decide you want something, move quickly with determination to get it done. Not only will you complete the task, you will move more quickly to realize it, which will exponentially jump you by leaps and bounds toward your goal. It is time to take massive, quick action and get cranking on the four steps. They will get you where you want to be.

Remember back in Chapter 3 when we talked about funding your emergency fund? We talked about various ways to get it done as quickly as you can, even if you had to sell some things online, just so you could see progress. When we see small victories, we are motivated to keep going.

Getting started is the hardest part, so stop wasting time. You have been living paycheck-to-paycheck long enough. You already know what it takes to survive; why not discover what it means to truly live? When you are willing to do what it takes to succeed, when you realize that it *is* possible to look out for your self-interest and no one loses in the process, everyone wins!

We win a life that was designed to give us what we deserve, not just what we need or want. So if you wish to reap a good harvest, you must plant in ways that are smart, manageable, and healthy. If you seek a good idea, you are going to find it, but discernment and discipline must weed out the multitude of bad ideas that may be flashier or provide temporary, fleeting happiness. When you picked up this book, you sought a good idea—and my four steps are proven to work. Get started. Do not wait a second longer.

One Bite at a Time

To paraphrase a famous quote from motivational speaker Zig Ziglar, if you give enough to many, you will receive everything you need and more. If you change, everything will change for you. When you set your first mini-goal, start with something that is easy and work hard at it. Quick, massive action will get you there. Your next mini-goal will not be quite as easy. The next one may cross the threshold of actually being difficult, but you are motivated by the success of the others. Smaller goals will achieve your bigger goal.

I have spent a lot of time reinforcing "quick, massive action," but the reality is that it is not sustainable. If it was, we would all be financially free in thirty days or less. The reason I like massive, quick action is because you see some immediate results, but you can't chip away at large amounts of debt all at once. It will take those small steps, starting with something easy and relatively painless so you do not get frustrated when you encounter a challenge that is far more difficult.

There will be times when you will want to give up. You are trying to live the way only 10 percent of the world does, not the other 90 percent. This means you will take a look around and see others living it up spending money they do not have, while you are tightening your belt. This is when you need to take a deep breath and ask yourself some questions that my life coach, Chel, tells me to ask myself each day:

- Who am I going to show up for today?
- What do I need to show up for today?
- Why is it important that I show up with the tools necessary to get the job done?

In fact, post these questions on your bathroom mirror, your dashboard, and your desk—as many places as you need to remind you over the next eighteen to twenty-four months that it will be worth it.

Is massive, quick action, more important than gradual progress? The two are not mutually exclusive; in fact, your quick action will be what jumpstarts you on your road to success. But no one can remain in massive action. That is when the slow, gradual process kicks in to take you further down the road (like the tortoise and the hare). Slow and steady wins the race; you will have periods where unexpected money comes to you, however, like a job bonus, raise, tax refund, or paid off debt. When that happens, jump back into massive, quick action with that money to tackle something with speed again. These cycles will help to keep you motivated, focused, and moving forward. After the quick start out of the gate, you are going to evolve into a gradual process of chugging up that hill, like the Little Engine that Could, which gets you to financial independence. But the beauty of this process is not what you *get*; it is what you *become*. When the stress of money loses its grip on your life, you can grow into the person you are supposed to be.

What About Setbacks?

Look, we live in a fallen world. It is not perfect by any means. This is a process done in steps. You will have setbacks, and your response to them will determine if your little engine chugs forward or hiccups backward. Think about that little engine chugging up the hill. She would lunge forward, maybe slip back, then gather more steam for another lunge up the hill, gaining more ground. There are always setbacks to achieving any goal; it is part of the process.

I remember when we had built up a big emergency fund, then suddenly I had to spend it on our house. The bay windows were sinking, and if left alone, they would pull our roof down. I had to spend my entire emergency fund to fix the problem. I did not want to, and it hurt, but that is why the fund was there. In fact, one of my friends whom I had helped get out of debt was the one who reminded me that is why it was there. I had just worked so hard to build it up, even though I knew I could build it up again, but gee whiz, it would be a challenge to get it back to where it was. Finally, I just said to myself, I have to do this (it is an emergency), then get back *on the train and start chugging away toward my goals and dreams.*

Address the setback, then jump right back in where you left off. You are going to have pitfalls and failures, and there might be an unexpected expense. As we talked about earlier, your emergency fund may not cover the entire expense, and you may have to finance the darn thing. But remember: *This is not a failure. It is a setback. You know what to do to get back on track.*

I love making myself to-do lists. They keep me focused and give me a sense of accomplishment each time I check off another task completed. My mother will ask me, "What have you done today?"

I always reply, "I did enough by noon to make a grown man cry." And I always say *man*—not woman.

Women are known for multitasking and getting the job done. My husband, Brad, is the greatest—he really is. All the girls in our family, even the in-laws, say they wish they had a Brad.

That said, there is just something about men in general: if you tell them three things that you need them to do, and they haven't written them down, you might as well forget it...because they already have. We discussed the chemicals that "wash" men's brains before birth in a previous chapter—men went out to kill the food and bring it back to the cave, while women managed all the other tasks. Hunting down the food took a while! To-do lists can help, though. I always left them for each of my children as they were growing up, and they arrived home before me. The delegating of a few tasks to each member of the family takes the load off of the one in charge. We have to remember this and stop being a martyr. I can't recommend this enough.

Let me encourage you to write a to-do list that is a series of small increments to get you to big goals for yourself and your family. This sort of visual will further motivate you to show up for yourself every day and give you benchmarks when you experience setbacks. It reminds you of why you are plugging away at your job each day and that your load will be lighter each time you cross off a task. Decide for yourself if your to-do list is a daily list, a weekly list, or a monthly list; in fact, I would encourage you to do all of the above, to keep you motivated each day, each week, each month. (And if necessary, buy yourself your own copy of *The Little Engine that Could*. I won't tell anyone, I promise.)

Sometimes, of course, you might need a small break. In our family we took little hiatuses when we needed a rest from keeping up and being so cognizant of every dollar spent. You might need a break every now or then, but then get right back on track and keep chugging toward your goals as soon as you can. When you reach a goal, eat at your favorite restaurant, or go to an amusement or water park that is close to you. Make sure you do not break the budget, and get right back on track.

If you linger too much on any setback, worry creeps in. You will start experiencing self-doubt, wondering if you'll ever get it sorted out. You might start wondering if you are delusional in thinking that you can get your finances in order. Do not let it become a full-blown worry. Get right back on track. Worry is one of the biggest diseases of attitude. There are negative forces in life, and this is normal. Our world is imperfect, so life will have its imperfections, flaws, and unfair experiences. We must learn how to handle the negative. Do not ignore it, but don't let it take up residency in your mind or heart, either. Allow it to surface, and send it on its way.

The great news is that evil is no match for good, but your good has to be active. Do not live with indecision; that only leads to wrong decisions. Decisions made early on will be what sets the course to change your life. You have been given information on how to change your family legacy, and now it is time to implement what you've learned.

In the book *The Richest Man in Babylon*, there is a story of a father who tried to direct his son to invest with a man whom he really trusted. The son listened but decided he had plenty of time to commit to his father's advice. He wanted to enjoy life with his new wife. Other investors took that father's advice, and ten years later they were living easier, more comfortable lives in comparison to the young man. So the son grew old and was still working hard day after day, never seeming to get ahead.

This story illustrates the power of compounding interest and why you will never regret saving and investing early and often for your future, especially when you get to the age of retirement. Doubt is like a plague, but self-doubt is the worst. We become timid and take a timid approach to life as a result.

Risk drives some people crazy, but everything is risky. The minute you were born, you entered a world of risk.

You might say, "I'm scared." If you are scared, we can lay you under a sheet on a bed and bring you three square meals a day, making sure nothing ever happens to you. You say "Yeah, but that is not living." Exactly—that is not living! The bottom line is that if you think trying is risky, wait until you get the bill for *not trying*. If you think investing is risky, wait until you see what not investing yields.

You were made to prosper and have joy. And when you understand this and the magnitude of your self-worth, it is the beginning of progress.

You gain insight that you can do anything you set your mind and effort to, but worry is one of insight's worst enemies. It causes health problems, which can take us off course. When we worry ourselves to the point that we have to focus on addressing specific physical or mental health issues, instead of simply maintaining good health, that is time that would otherwise be put toward accomplishing our goals. We can't change anything with worry. We can, however, change so many things with defined goals, laser focus, and effort.

Life is a bundle of good and bad experiences that make you who you are and make you even better for your next decision. Do not be the pessimistic person who writes to me and says, "Oh my gosh, I read your book. And I know five reasons why this would never work." Well, hello sister, you only need one reason to stay "safe" on the sidelines with the other 90 percent who don't dare. (And P.S. They don't sleep at night, because they don't know how they will make the mortgage next month.)

I have presented you with tools that work to get the job done, but you have to actively engage them. You can keep looking through the picture window, or you can be outside in the sunshine. Our lives are mostly influenced by the way we think. Poor thinking habits keep people poor.

Your mind is a mental factory into which you pour what your life is about. Setbacks will come, and you get to decide whether you will backslide or keep chugging forward. Pew research shows wealthy people read seventeen books or more a year. Bill Gates reads fifty books a year, or about one book *per week*. Earlier this year, Gates told *Time* magazine that reading books for over an hour a day was a critical ingredient of his success. "Every book teaches me something new or helps me see things differently," Gates said. "Reading fuels a sense of curiosity about the world, which I think helped drive me forward in my career."

The wealthy do not just sit back and roll around in their money. They continue to learn and read and grow. This is how you open your mind to new opportunities and information. And this is how you become the interesting person that sparks interest in another person who might assist you with a great business opportunity or a different job. Building a good life is not easy or simple; you must be wise and careful about how you think. Negative thinking and self-doubt can do a lot of damage, especially to your bank account.

If you do not like your current job, you can move up or find a different one. Stop wasting time complaining about it or nitpicking every wrong it has ever brought you. Even if the pay is good, do not sit there counting your days until retirement. You may not live long enough to see it, so why waste more years in the exact same spot?

You have been given a four-step guide to getting your life on a totally different track from where most people are headed. You are tired of where you are and want a different life for yourself and your family. Now is the time to work hard and put that plan into action. Trust me, if I can do this, you can do this. And I *did*.

Each day has enough trouble of its own; why add worry to it? You have made it through every trial that you've faced so far. You will make it through this one. Strike while the iron is hot—make these decisions with momentum and passion:

- Decide to work the four steps.

- Commit to them for the long term.

- Resolve that you will not let any setbacks put you on the sidelines.

The 2 Percent Difference

I have a saying, "Think long, think wrong." What I mean by that is when you waste too much time making a decision, you will wind up never taking action. After you read this book, you may not jump in and immediately do everything I have advised. You should spend a little time crafting a strategy to get moving, but do not linger there. Two percent of people will usually act on great knowledge that they receive. It does not matter the area of improvement we are discussing. They will go buy the book, read the entire book, and implement its strategies. You are on your way to being in that 2 percent! Even imperfect action is still action. And that is the 2 percent difference.

Some people plan out everything to the *n*th degree. Instead, think about what you can do *right now*. *Right this very second*. Need some ideas?

- Set up an Excel spreadsheet for your budget.

- Jumpstart your emergency fund with an old jar and use it to dump your spare change (you'd be surprised how quickly it will add up).

- Pack your lunch to take with you to work tomorrow.

- Set your thermostat lower in the winter and higher in the summer. Bundle up if you're cold, strip off layers if you're hot.

Whatever action you take, it will get you closer to your goal. Keep plugging away at the mini-goals to get you to the big goal.

They say you have to do something ten thousand hours to become an expert at it. I say, do not waste time—take action now and chip away at those hours. Every day, revisit your to-do lists. This is really how you become an expert on finances. It is time to start working on the four steps and making it a reality for your household. If you do something consistently for a long time, you are hard-wiring it into your mind, and you will be able to help so many people in the future.

Do what is right, and keep doing it. This is why the 2 percent difference matters—you will discover what works, and your confidence will increase. The next thing you know, you have done what is right for a long time, which makes you an expert. It also makes you the standard others will want to achieve. How many world records took decades to achieve—and once someone finally did it, others realized they could do it, too? After Roger Bannister broke the four-minute mile in 1954, many runners started breaking it, too. Since then, over 1,400 athletes have broken the record. When others see that someone else has accomplished something, they are motivated because they know it is possible. Make yourself a beacon of light to show others that they can be part of the 2 percent difference, too. Figure out how you are going to do it, and have faith that you know how to produce the certainty of a positive outcome.

If you want to win at finances, you have to stop wasting time and start the plan. Stop all the time wasters that have a chokehold on your mind, telling you that your dreams are not attainable. I often have people tell me that they have tried everything to get out of debt or lose weight. No, they haven't. They have tried *something*—but not everything.

I have given you a plan. If it is implemented, it will work. I am asking you to take eighteen to twenty-four months of your life to end up living the best version of your life. Get excited, get motivated, act quickly, and get going before the feeling passes. Before you talk yourself out of it. Before fear creeps in and immobilizes you. Do not fear success.

There is a domino effect that can either be positive or negative. Your thoughts tip the first domino, but you are in control of the direction. Choose wisely, but *choose to act*—it affects everything else. Believe it, visualize it, and work hard for it. That is how you get it. You will still encounter hardships along the way—everyone does. You will still reach your goals more quickly with positive thinking, and the process will be much more enjoyable. This attitude will allow you to enjoy every step of your journey.

Use this book as a starting block to make your dreams come true. It is an easy, kitchen-table approach to managing your finances. These steps do build on each other, but they are all independently and equally important to your goal of financial freedom.

Find Some Backup

There are going to be those times when you need extra support. A bad day or a perfect storm of setbacks kicks in and you want to throw in the towel. So as you plan your strategy for financial freedom, make sure you also have some backup in the form of an accountability partner. You are going to need backup on days where you're ready to give up.

Think about who your head cheerleader might be, someone who can help to reinforce why you are doing this and encourage you to stay in the game.

Likely, your closest friends immediately come to mind, but let me caution you here. Your biggest cheerleaders, at least when it comes to finances, may not be your "besties." Some might say, "You are not poor, why would you want to live like this, even for a short time?" or "You make good money, and everyone has debt!"

People will be jealous of you, or scoff at your efforts and tell you what you're doing is dumb. Part of this is because they themselves do not want to put in the effort and are jealous that you will leave them behind. Others will dismiss you as being "too money hungry." This is not true; quite the opposite. You no longer want to be burdened by a bank, a finance company, a mortgage company, a landlord, a credit card balance, and debt.

Be very selective about your head cheerleader; choose wisely, thinking through who would get resentful if you canceled weekly coffee or lunch plans in lieu of less-expensive alternatives. Think through whether someone would be hurt that your holiday gifts are not as extravagant, instead of feeling happy you thought of them. Which friend would not only be excited for your steps, but might also actually *initiate* or suggest ways your get-togethers could be more budget-friendly?

An accountability partner might be a mentor or a coach who can help you find your way back after backsliding. You also need somebody to root you on, especially if you don't have another adult in the house, or the other adult is not quite on board with what you are wanting to do. In the beginning, Brad wasn't exactly on board, but when he saw results, he came around. So even if you have a partner or spouse who is not as gung ho as you, don't rule out their enthusiasm further down the road, but you need a cheerleader *now*.

If you really don't have anyone who can serve as backup, try to invent a small reward system. Maybe something you gave up in order to build your emergency fund? Like, if you followed the plan for six months, you could get one professional pedicure instead of making do with your homemade version. Or purchase a pound of the fancy coffee from the fancy coffeehouse where you used to get your morning coffee (that is one way to stretch the reward instead of hitting the coffeehouse for a one-and-done!) Splurge on a babysitter and enjoy a glass of wine in your backyard or at a friend's house for grownup conversation. Keep it small, but reward yourself for a job well done and to keep you motivated to stay the course of action.

Remember, this takes time and the journey is what makes you who you are. Discipline yourself to stay positive, no matter who you are around; do not go down the rabbit hole with them. You can also watch too much news and spend too much time on social media. If scary things are going on, which they usually are, this is negative overload, and you can infect yourself with it, so take an occasional break and go off-the-grid to keep your focus. When you experience setbacks, do not dwell on them.

To Everything There Is a Season

I know that I sound like a broken record, but this is just a season of your life—it is not forever. You are devoting eighteen to twenty-four months to save as much as you can in a reasonable amount of time to get debts paid, but you do this in balance with everything else, not at the sacrifice of relationships or family time.

Benjamin Franklin said that happiness does not come from big pieces of great success, but from small advantages hammered out day by day. So let's be happy with what we have while we are in pursuit of what we want. Place no contingencies or conditions on this. Do not think, *If I just had _____, I would be happy* (even if the thought is to be debt-free). When our happiness is conditional like that, we will often neglect what is happening in the present and miss out on a good portion of our lives.

Abraham Lincoln said, "You will be as happy as you make up your mind to be right now." Be happy along the way. It does not mean that you can't or shouldn't aim for great things, but enjoy the journey. Take pride in your accomplishments, and do not equate ambition with greed. Make sure that your ambition is housed within the desire to do better and succeed.

The next year and a half to two years is a season. You will not always be struggling, and in fact, you may discover that you are not struggling at all. It *is* possible to work the four steps and enjoy life at the same time. It may feel like a long winter, but I promise you that spring is just around the corner.

No matter where you are today, no matter the status of your finances at the very hour you are reading this, *you need to start saving money.* You need to have a little socked away so that you can stay within your budget and pay off debt. Then you need to save a little more. We have talked about the power of compounding interest. It works at *any* age.

Living below your means allows you freedom. It is like taking that deep breath at the ocean on a sunny day, or wherever your happy place may be. It is pure peace, and once you have been able to inhale and exhale to that extent, you can move forward with confidence and truly live. You can be a blessing to others because much of the stress in this life revolves around not having enough money to do the things or help the people we want to. Having achieved the four steps, you no longer have those barriers. As you help others, create teachable moments for your children, and expand your generosity. You are creating a legacy that compounds as much as the interest in your retirement account. Can you feel that in your soul? That is my hope for you.

Always Be a Blessing

Even if you are choked with financial debt, you're not meant to be an average person who just lives paycheck-to-paycheck. You are meant to have peace and freedom. We are learning that we hold the keys to our own freedom and that we do not have to be slaves to the lender. Once we are free, we can pursue our passions.

You might not be able to pursue your true passion right now, but you are working toward your freedom, and you can find things to be passionate about in the meantime. Maybe it is simply shifting your attitude about your current job, recognizing that it is a means to an end to get you financially free. Or perhaps you have had a small epiphany about losing the taste for extravagance, now that you've seen what saving does for the soul. Shiny things lose their luster. When we wait, it makes special occasions even more meaningful.

The title of this chapter is "Stop Wasting Time," and that includes not waiting to be a blessing to someone else. We have talked a bit about generosity, legacies, and teachable moments, but let's connect the dots to all of it. We can always help, even if it is in small ways. We can always give our time, talent, and yes, resources. There is always going to be someone in worse shape than we are, whether it is physical, mental, emotional, spiritual, or financial.

Think of someone where you work who is largely ignored. Nobody knows his name or his story. Maybe she cleans your office or he delivers the mail. Make a point to be the exception. Offer them a cold bottle of water on hot days or hot coffee on cold days. Address them by their name, ask how they are doing, and really listen when they talk. Ask questions. When you see them in passing, call them by name and say hello. If someone is with you, introduce them.

You do not have to sit frozen and continue to waste time on your own guilt because you have no idea how you can even pay your bills this month. If you did not have to worry about money, take a moment to think about what that would feel like. Own this feeling, and live courageously thinking about it. Find ways to pull that feeling into the present tense as you discover ways to bless others. Write down some of these so you can refer to your list on days that don't go so well, and remember to write down how you felt. You might be surprised at what is most fulfilling to you.

If you do not act, I guarantee that your life will be decided for you. You will continue living paycheck-to-paycheck, emergency-to-emergency, and stressed out. You will probably be holding your breath a lot of the time, which physically keeps your heart rate and cortisol levels really high, which hurts your organs and your whole body. I would be remiss if I pretended to forget about the medical side of this.

We spend our whole lives waiting on the next big thing. What we need to realize sooner rather than later is that the next big thing will not make us any happier when we get there, not long term anyway. I have been through a lot of those little milestones myself. When we really concentrate on enjoying the process and learn to be content with what we have, that frees us to take in each moment—and these moments *are* our lives. The choices we are making, those little small choices every day, is what makes our life. No matter what our happiness level is right now, we can always choose joy. If you stop wasting time, one thing is for certain: your life will change on *your* terms.

WANNA HAVE FUND$?

What is the one thing you could do this week to propel yourself toward your goals more quickly? Stop wasting time—do it!

Conclusion

I DO NOT JUST COUNSEL OTHERS USING THE FOUR STEPS. I HAVE ACTUALLY *lived* the steps.

A lot of what you have been reading is actually my trial-and-error story. I know what it's like to fall short before the next payday. I know what it's like to lose a father while he was still young, to have a teenage pregnancy, to go through an unwanted divorce, and to be single and struggling—with all sorts of odds stacked against me. I know what it's like to have a good job with good pay, and still be unable to afford a pizza.

I also know what it's like to say enough is enough and make big changes. To persist when you would rather give up. To cast a wide net to learn how to fix your finances and realize through trial and error that everyone's situation is unique and there is no "one-size-fits-all" formula that magically gets you in the black overnight. I also realized I am not alone in these circumstances, and there are others out there who need a large dose of hope, grace, and encouragement.

Thankfully, I have realized many new things and have emerged on the other side of financial captivity to find the freedom and peace that eludes so many of us today. I have overcome the odds stacked against me and taken ownership of some of the bad circumstances that I got myself into. I have also released the things that were out of my control. They are all part of what we call *life*. I now have four kids—almost all of them through college—a nicely funded retirement, and I am debt-free. I could stop right here, retire in just a few years, and live very comfortably, thanks and good night. My heart, however, has made other plans.

For some time, my heart has been telling me that I have to share my story and help others do the same thing that I've done. I want to reach people and help them become financially free, find success, and get their lives back. I want to pay it forward. If you had told twenty-two-year-old me that Future Me would be counseling others on getting their finances in order, I would have probably laughed.

You see, if I can do this, then anyone can. I have been there and can identify with the shame, guilt, and confusion about personal finances. To paraphrase a favorite passage of scripture, why is it that I do what I do not want to do? And those things I want to do, I do not do?

I think human nature is to have that desire. However, it is the follow-through, patience, and discipline that can trip us up. We know we should eat right, get plenty of exercise, and drink water, but we backslide. And when we do, which is frequently, we joke about how we will start all that "tomorrow."

How are you using your time, relationships, and money? I want to help you get the life you always dreamed of. And I know this works. I work in medicine, and some patients respond to my health suggestions positively, but most will nod, smile, and resume their life just as they have lived it so far. We have talked about living in the 10 percent, and my job as a financial counselor is to convince you, just like my patients, to do what will be best for you in your waking hours. Beyond reading this book, I want you to achieve your desired goals. I usually only get fifteen or twenty minutes with my patients, but my readers can continue to refer back to these pages, time and again.

Right now, your brain wants to keep you in your comfort zone, even if it is not working for you, even if your life is not working for you, because the brain tries to help you conserve energy. It is in the business of self-preservation. The brain wants to keep you paralyzed by telling you why this will be a lot of work. By keeping you there, you are not having to exercise it. My job is to show you a better life and get you out of your comfort zone so you can do what is really best for you and your family.

If you can break that barrier, then we are going to get to the good stuff. In fact, you could complete the four-step process and have peace for the rest of your life without stretching your brain beyond that. But here is the interesting part: If you continue, you can change your family's financial dynamics for generations to come. You can change how your kids, your grandkids, and those further down the line will be affected. Each person has to do what they feel is best in their life. Now that you have a taste of what you *can* do and, more importantly, what you can do without—a weighty yoke of debt and overspending—it can take on a snowball effect that you can build on. That requires continuous action over time.

Here is the bottom line: You can study and research all the financial plans out there. But the simple answer is that you need to pick a plan. You must get the debt paid off in order to free up some money. As money is applied to other debt, you will free up more money. I do not encourage anyone to stop there, because the money that is freed up can be put to good use.

If you start investing for retirement, for example, your life is going to be so much better and secure. Peace is going to flow down on you. You will be a better steward of what has been entrusted to you. You will see more blessings, and you will be able to share your abundance with others. This is what *really* makes me tick.

You will lose much of your taste for buying things after you learn to pay cash for them, find great deals on the things you want, and have your life in order. A finer point is that you can afford some nicer things now, without bringing the stress home along with them.

The Four Steps: Quick Review

Let's review what we've learned: consider this your "cheat sheet" to use however you wish, as long as it keeps you tracking in the right direction!

Step One: Build an emergency fund. It is a lifesaver. You will have it when you need it.

An emergency fund is so important. Many unexpected expenses happen in life, and when we have not prepared, they can wreck a budget. When that happens, you are right back in credit card debt or financing something to handle it. You are digging out of that hole—do not slide back into it. In time, you are going to return to the emergency fund again and again, making it even more robust.

Try to visualize yourself sitting on top of a fire engine, on guard, ready to soak any problems with the hose of your emergency fund. Visualize taming big fires, making them into smaller fires. If it is a really big fire, you will have to get the whole cavalry involved. But as long as you've got that fire engine and the hose ready, you can still make it a smaller fire so that it is extinguished more quickly.

Step Two: Develop a budget. When you budget, it actually means that you are telling your money where to go. Every dollar and bill should be accounted for in your budget. Don't worry about what the money is going to be assigned to, just figure out *where* it is going. Then decide if that is where you want it to go.

If you give every dollar that comes into your house a name, things will start building quickly. Remember, *budget* does not mean doing without—it means you decide what you want to spend it on.

So many people just do not have a plan, and they continue living paycheck-to-paycheck, thinking that is all there is. That is not all there is. If you are willing to work and put the time in, you can do anything you want.

Many people despise the word *budget*, conjuring up ideas that it is too restrictive and that they will have no fun. Instead, try to visualize yourself as the big boss of your money, whatever take you have on the phrase *big boss*. Maybe to you, it means you are sitting with your arms crossed on a stack of it, discerning and directing where each dollar should go.

Step Three: Use the debt locomotive. My favorite strategy when it comes to debt reduction is paying off the smallest balances first. With this approach, you can see some real progress in a shorter amount of time. Once it is paid off, you can rename that amount and tell it to go toward the next smallest debt. As you pay off each one, you free up more money and gain momentum, like the Little Engine that Could. As your debt locomotive grabs steam, it climbs that hill, finally gets you over the top, and you coast into a place of financial freedom. This is my hope for you.

You do not know what this feels like until you get there, but the only way I can describe it is *priceless*. This is the main reason I feel compelled to share what I have learned with others. I want the financial floodgates to open for you, giving you a peace that surpasses all understanding. So climb aboard already!

Visualize yourself as the engineer on the train, cresting the hill. Feel the wind gently blowing through your hair as you coast to freedom.

Step Four: Plan for retirement. When you get ready to retire, you will want to enjoy it. No matter how much people love you, they will not be able to support you during your retirement. You would not want that life, anyway, where you are dependent on someone else's money to get you through.

Start contributing to a retirement account as early as you can and let the magic of compounding interest propel you to an enjoyable, peaceful retirement. It is never too late to start saving.

When I think of retirement, I think of the phrase *easy street*. If we do not name some of our dollars *Retirement*, they are named for us: *Thoughtless Spending*. We sometimes buy stuff and we don't even get it out of the box for a year. There are so many things to want in this world, and many of these temporary pleasures can rob you of your retirement. Be selective and thoughtful about each dollar's name, and be sure some of them are named Retirement. Retirement comes anyway, so prepare for it a little bit each day so you can stop working for pay and pursue the desires of your heart. Now is your time to give back like never before and leave a legacy.

Let's visualize using the phrase *living on easy street*. When you read that phrase, what comes to mind? I visualize myself running on the beach, looking at palm trees, feeling the waves hit my feet. The setting is peaceful, and my heart is peaceful, too, because this scene, this vacay, is already paid off. What does the phrase *living on easy street* conjure up for you?

What You Do *Now* Matters

Think about the legacy you want to leave and write it down. Remember that you can do this; it makes you who you are and how you will be remembered now and for generations. There may be setbacks, but keep moving forward and think about the future you want and how you will make the world better while you are here (and beyond).

I have made a big deal about giving, because giving is a big deal. I totally believe in the flat, open hand, not the clenched fist. This will allow money to flow in and out of your life as needed. They call it *currency* for a reason. Holding on to some of it is fine, but if you hold it too tightly, more money can't come in as needed.

If your paycheck is eaten up with your expenses, however, do not get discouraged; your giving may not include money at this time. It may mean giving a portion of your willing, generous heart. It may mean giving your time. (And speaking of time, the time will come when you will be in a better position to give money. You will get there.)

It may mean that you give a listening ear. It may mean that you write get-well cards to people, take a meal to someone, tell someone that you will pray for them—*and then actually do it*. There is always a neighbor who needs their yard raked or mowed. Bake cookies and take them to someone. Do you know that there are many people in the United States who do not get a single smile during the day? Yet when someone gives us one, we are drawn to them, at least for a moment, because they took the time to notice us.

If you are a practicing Christian and feel guilt and shame over not being able to tithe (literally, meaning give 10 percent of your income to support *His* work), don't sweat it. God says give with a grateful heart—not one that is fearful. Give what you can with a grateful heart.

Do not let guilt control your life and keep you from taking action. This stress used to wake me up at night. I have operated so much of my life on guilt. I wish I could do it over, but I have allowed guilt to control many of my decisions. I read a book suggested by my friend Steph called *The Pressure's Off* by Larry Crabb, which helped me start the journey of rejecting guilt. Do not let giving cause you stress; *giving* can mean a lot of different things and can be accomplished in a variety of ways. Pick a way to give now that will work in your life with your goals.

I've Checked All the Boxes—Now What?

You've completed the four steps and have gotten over the hill of financial insecurity. So now do you relax? Do you stop, or do you continue setting new goals?

First, find a way to celebrate this tremendous turning point. When I finally got there, I stopped and rested for a little, but I got right back on track. I set new goals and kept right on chugging. I avoid impulsive spending and want each purchase to have some thought behind it. If we dip into our emergency fund for any reason, we hit a reset button and rebuild that first. We do not incur any major expenses or purchases unless it is an emergency, like the refrigerator breaks or you are fixing the furnace.

Frankly, I have lost my taste for a lot of things, and I save for the other things that I want. For example, we like to take our entire family—grandchildren and all—on paid-for trips to Florida, where we rent a large beach house and enjoy being together. Those are the sorts of wishlist "things" that we save for *now*—meaningful experiences and memories in the making, the things that add value to life.

Retirement has always been a big issue for me, so I have saved as much as I could. I did not ever want to be a burden to someone else. I knew that in the year I turned fifty, I could do catch-up contributions, so I have plugged away at each step toward retirement. While I am not sure at this point that I will ever "retire" in a traditional sense, I will be able to be generous and help others when I no longer require a paycheck.

When you hit some specific goals, I think it just changes your mind-set. You start thinking, *Now what can I do?* instead of *What do I have to do?* When you can give your money freely and with gratitude, there is no drug, drink, or material possession that matches the feeling that comes with it.

If you decide to relax permanently, having finished Step Four, you will still be head and shoulders above a lot of people, but for myself, I have elected not to stay there. I still ask for wisdom and direction on the best use of my money. God does not care if you spend some money on yourself and enjoy it—it is all about your heart. Having been through this myself, I can attest that my heart has been changed.

Get Moving!

Are you fed up enough yet? Are you tired of not knowing whether you will make ends meet this month? Are you weary of robbing Peter to pay Paul? Are you disgusted enough with your current financial situation? Good!

The time is ripe for you to find some inspiration. Reading this book or learning about how other people did it, bringing themselves back from the brink of bankruptcy, are great resources. It helps when others have blazed the trail for you. As you say to yourself, *They did it. Can I?*

then you respond, *I think I can, I think I can.* Just like the Little Engine that Could. It is one thing to hear about others' experiences, but finding the desire deep within yourself to change takes this to an entirely new level. Someone's experience will resonate with yours and trigger it. You will know it when the trigger says, *It is time to make a change and live differently now so that I can live differently later.* It is time to do what others won't do now, so I can have what others don't have later.

If you are fed up, find sources of inspiration to trigger your own desire for change. I hope this book is one of them. In order to get moving and keep moving, you must resolve that this is it, once and for all, do or die. You are going to stick with it no matter what, even if it requires a lot of trial and error (which it will). Resolve not to give up until you find something that works for you.

Results are the name of the game. Let's get to work on producing more than you need for yourself so that you can share with others, your community, and your nation. Give some away, and remember to be thankful for what you already have.

We have so much in this country. There are eternal "laws" of wealth that say those who wish to be the greatest will find a way to be of service to many. It is now time for you to be of service to yourself and your family, then expand on that.

I have talked quite a bit about visualization and the ability to see things that do not yet exist. Can you see yourself where you want to be? You must learn to visualize, then take massive, quick action for impact. The quicker you get started, the more likely you are going to succeed.

Many people read good information. They feel affected by it, but they never put it into action. Do not let this happen to you. You have some great information packed into these four simple steps. Go put them into practice and keep doing that until you succeed. And you know what? You will. Do not be scared to create wealth; it is not bad in and of itself. It is the *love* of money that is the problem. If you are being generous with the money you earn, you do not love it in the wrong way.

Wealth is a magnifier. It just magnifies what is already there and who you already are. Make sure you are a high-quality person by working harder on yourself than you do on your job, and doing these steps. You will be the person you want to be, and when the wealth shows up, the money will allow you to help others instead of being self-centered—it is your choice.

Your thoughts are very important in getting where you want to go. So use them wisely. Do not just go for low-hanging fruit; keep climbing higher. When you get to the top of the tree, *all* the fruit is yours, not just the fruit at the bottom. If we focus on why we are here and what we are meant to do, the rest of it will come.

Each moment of every day is made up of small choices that comprise your life. Anyone can buy a car they love, but there is always going to be a better car. It is not what you get that makes you valuable. It is your character and heart that make you valuable. Your character grows during each battle that you overcome.

It is not just in the goal and attaining it; it is how you get there that really counts. If you fall a little short, you are still going to land on your feet. I say shoot for the sun! Even if you fall short, you're still going to end up under a palm tree on the beach, looking at the ocean. And that's not so bad, right?

I hope you'll drop me a line: @AuthorMonicaAllen.

Additional Resources

- See if there is a financial group at your church or a Meetup group that focuses on personal finances (or start your own, with some solid content!)

- Look into community colleges that offer low- or no-cost seminars and classes.

- Search out consumer credit counselors, just make sure that there is no fee involved. A consumer credit counselor is different from debt consolidators or debt reduction services.

- Read all that you can—don't just take one person's advice.

- YouTube and other sites have a ton of content on how credit works and how to be a responsible consumer, and they can keep you motivated.

MONTHLY BUDGET						
	Income - 1					
	Income - 2					
Expenses	BUDGET					
Mortgage / Rent						
Church / Tithe						
Car Payment						
Insurance/House/Car						
Life Insurance						
Child Support						
Savings						
Allowance/Spend ⊠						
Electric/Water/Trash						
Gas/Fuel/House						
Water / Garbage						
Telephone						
Gas /Auto Expenses						
Food ⊠						
Eat Out ⊠						
Snack & Lunch						
Personal						
Childcare						
Household ⊠						
Clothes						
Medical/Dental						
School / Lunch						
Recreation / Cable						
Haircuts ⊠						
Extra $ Towards Debt						
Internet						
Total =						
Envelope Money ⊠						

Left vertical labels: Fixed Amounts, Fixed Variable, Occasional

⊠ = Those categories we used cash for

DEBT LOCOMOTIVE

Item	Total Payoff	Minimum Payment	New Payment

Acknowledgments

My son, Brandon Allen, gets the credit for the book cover design and all inserts throughout the book. I love the book cover! He certainly caught my vision. My dear friend Chel Garrison gets the credit for all photos, including the book cover. Your wisdom and encouragement have helped me go where I need to! I want to thank all of my children, Ashley, Brandon, Logan, and Josh, for the life experiences that helped us all grow, learn, and get stronger together. Their spouses, Blake, Erica, Mallorie, and Meghan have added joy and completeness to our family. I cannot forget to mention the pure love and happiness that my grands Brooklyn, Madison (Madi), and Theo have added to our lives! Who knew?! My husband Brad has helped me build this life that we love, giving endless support; he is definitely my 'wingman.' You are all my loves and everything I do is ultimately for you and our legacy.

A big thanks to Scribe Publishing for helping me through this process, and Miriam Drennan who held my hand through the long hours of writing. A book takes a village and I have the best!

Most of all, I want to thank God who has given me the vision and perseverance to use my gifts to help others.